Information Governance and Assurance

Reducing risk, promoting policy

Alan MacLennan

facet publishing

© Alan MacLennan 2014

Published by Facet Publishing
7 Ridgmount Street, London WC1E 7AE
www.facetpublishing.co.uk

Facet Publishing is wholly owned by CILIP:
the Chartered Institute of Library and Information
Professionals.

British Library Cataloguing in Publication Data
A catalogue record for this book is available from the
British Library.

ISBN 978-1-85604-940-5

First published 2014

Text printed on FSC accredited material.

Typeset from author's files in 10.5/15pt New Baskerville
and Frutiger by Flagholme Publishing Services.
Printed and bound by CPI Group (UK) Ltd, Croydon, CR0 4YY

Contents

Acknowledgements

Thanks to Blue, who helped me with the modular bit, Jacqui, Eilidh and Fiona for putting up with me during the writing and Jenni Hall for being such an encouraging editor.

Alan MacLennan

Acronyms and abbreviations

ALA: American Library Association
AUP: Acceptable Use Policy
BCMS: Business Continuity Management System
BPR: Business Process Re-engineering
BSI: British Standards Institute
CILIP: Chartered Institute of Library and Information Professionals
CMS: Content Management System
Commission: authors of a risk management tool
COSO: Committee of Sponsoring Organizations of the Treadway
  Commission, authors of a risk management tool
CPSR: Local Authorities (England) Charges for Property Searches
  Regulations
CRM: Customer Relationship Management
CRUD: Create, Retrieve, Update, Delete (the basic operations on a
  database)
DDoS: Distributed Denial of Service (a means of disabling a server)
DM: Disaster Management
DMZ: Demilitarized Zone (a sophisticated alternative to the simpler
  firewall)
DPA: Data Protection Act 1998 (UK)
DSS: Decision Support System
EC: European Community
EIR: Environmental Information Regulations (UK)
EPP: Enterprise Resource Planning
FOIA: Freedom of Information Act 2000 (UK)
FOISA: Freedom of Information (Scotland) Act 2002

FSA: Financial Services Authority (UK)

FSCS: Financial Services Compensation Scheme (UK)

GPS: Global Positioning System (allows devices to be located by satellite)

ICFR: Internal Control on Financial Reporting

ICO: Information Commissioner's Office (UK)

IEC: International Electrotechnical Commission

ILMS: Integrated Library Management System

IPR: Intellectual Property Rights

ISG: Information Security Governance

ISO: International Organization for Standardization

Jisc: Joint Information Systems Committee (UK)

MIS: Management Information Systems

MySQL: a popular open-source database management system

NARA: National Archives and Records Administration (US)

NASA: National Aeronautics and Space Administration (US)

NCOA: National Change of Address register (UK and US)

NRS: National Readership Survey (UK)

OCLC: Online Computer Library Center, Inc.

PAF: Postcode Address File (UK)

PCAOB: Public Company Accounting Oversight Board (established by the Sarbanes-Oxley Act)

PDF: Portable Document Format (a document file format)

SAR: Subject Access Request (under the Data Protection Act)

TNA: The National Archive (UK)

TPS: Transaction Processing Systems

Glossary of terms

Bandwidth: the 'carrying capacity' of a network connection, usually measured in bits per second

Botnet: a collection of computers, usually under the control of malware, which are used to attack a server, e.g. in a DDoS attack

Cloud computing: 'distributed' computing, in which storage, software, or computing platforms are provided remotely across a network

Cracking: 'breaking into' systems with malicious intent, such as data theft

Data: raw facts; unlabelled, unclassified

Data set: a collection of data about a particular topic, e.g. census returns, customer records, or invoices for a period

Firewall: a means of protecting a computer or network from intrusion. May be implemented in software or hardware

Framework: a conceptual structure used to categorize parts of a complex entity

Hacking: originally, creative experimentation with computers or software, intended to extend their utility. Now often conflated with cracking

Malware: software intended to harm, or interfere with, the operation of a computer. Includes viruses and Trojans

Metadata: meaningful labels applied to data, e.g. catalogue records, classifications, categories

Microsoft Access: a proprietary database management system

Oracle: a proprietary database management system

Pareto principle: the idea that a small proportion of something has a disproportionately large effect (e.g. '80% of the problems are caused by 20% of the code')

Patch: a release of software intended to rectify a fault in a particular version of a program

Protocol: what is 'expected' by a computer. This might be a username and password (close to the derivation of the term) or a particular communications convention like the 'dotted quad' Internet Protocol address scheme (e.g. 192.68.0.0)

Sarbanes-Oxley Act: the Public Company Accounting Reform and Investor Protection Act of 2002, which introduced strict controls on US organizations

Phishing: soliciting information, often usernames and passwords, usually via faked e-mails purporting to be from, e.g., a bank

Social engineering: soliciting information, often usernames and passwords, usually via telephone calls purporting to be from, e.g., an IT department

Spyware: software which monitors activity on a computer (e.g. websites visited) and transmits it back to the originator

Trojan: a type of malware which appears to be useful, but also does something harmful

Virus: a program which can replicate itself across networks or via removable storage, and which usually harms the 'infected' computer

Warez: software of dubious legality, e.g. 'cracked' versions of proprietary programs, where the registration key has been disabled, or fake keys to achieve the same effect

Worm: a program which replicates itself to other hosts on a network. Usually, though not always, harmful, if only due to wasted bandwidth

CHAPTER 1

Introduction

Rationale

'Information governance' describes the activities and practices which have developed around people's attempts to control the use of information, including, but not limited to, practices mandated by law. If we create a records management policy for an organization, we apply information governance principles. When legislatures pass laws to protect our personal information, they are attempting to enforce good information governance. At a personal level, good practices regarding password selection for online resources, or encryption of sensitive data, can constitute information governance. In a world in which information is increasingly seen as a top-level asset, the safeguarding and management of information is of concern to everyone.

Because information and its uses pervade our lives, it is important that it is handled efficiently. Because of increasing concerns regarding access to information, and regarding the consequences of misuse of information, there is a growing body of legislation worldwide which applies to the collection, storage, use and disposal of information. There is also a growing concern regarding the ethical use of information, and there is pressure on those handling information to be able to demonstrate that their handling of information meets ethical standards.

These factors are relevant to all involved in information work, from the researcher who is responsible for ethical practices in the gathering, analysis and storage of data to the reference librarian who must deliver unbiased information; from the records manager who must respond to information requests to the administrator handling personnel files.

Since aspects of information governance permeate information work, it is important that students in the information professions are aware of, and are equipped to implement, good practice in a wide range of areas of application.

The aim of this book is to present information governance as the key to the successful integration of the information professions with the organizations which they serve, with the interests of the individual and with society at large.

Data and information

The terms 'data' and 'information' were both used in the last section – there is some overlap in the meanings commonly given to the two terms, and this may result in confusion, because often they are used interchangeably. Here, 'data' is used in the sense of 'raw data' – the words, numbers, sounds, images which become information, once they are given a context – once they are labelled, or, in the language of the profession, once they have metadata applied to them.

A piece of research will often involve the collection of data – for example, the date of birth, gender, body mass index and calorie consumption of each of a sample group of participants in a dietary study. Each of these facts is a 'datum' – a 'given', and 'data', the plural form, are unlabelled facts, which can be turned into 'information' by setting them in context, and using them together with other data. A list of calorie consumptions becomes more informative – it supplies information – when matched to the other factors about the individuals concerned. A list of journey times is useless but, when combined with route details, and times of day they were recorded, might be used to make deductions about congestion on the route, for example.

Information as an asset

It has become something of a commonplace to say that an organization's most valuable asset is people, or employees, or its workforce, and this is presented in respect of the contribution made by their creativity, their energy, their vision, and the fact that people are central to the performance of any operation. However, in order to function effectively, even at the simplest tasks, people require information. This might range from the low-level procedures to manufacture and assemble components, to the management information which influences high-level strategic decision-making. The upsurge of interest in 'big data' has brought closer to the public consciousness the fact that organizations acquire vast quantities of data during their normal operations, and that previously unimaginable business advantages might lie in exploiting these data, by transforming them into management information, given the knowledge and facilities to do so.

One of the surest indicators of the value of information must be the lengths and expense to which individuals and organizations will go to obtain information which does not belong to them, with the intention of using it to their own advantage. Information theft, and its personal analogue, identity theft, have soared in frequency since the arrival of ubiquitous networking of information, and it is at this level that information governance impacts on us all.

Almost any interaction in which we take part generates an electronic trace. Some of these, like simple cash transactions in a shop, are anonymous, but if you use a store loyalty card, a debit or credit card, a mobile phone, a computer, a library card, or any one of an increasing number of identifiable media, your identity can be attached to transactions which are in themselves of interest to the data aggregator, but are potentially much more interesting as part of your electronic 'presence'. What you bought, and when and where, what else you bought at the same time, how these items are placed in that particular shop, what is currently being advertised on media that you use – all these and more are grist to the 'big data' mill.

However, when we become identifiable from the information that is stored about us, restrictions are placed – most would agree, quite properly – on what may be done with the information, and how it may be handled. These restrictions, and associated pieces of legislation, will be covered in Chapter 2, but in this chapter it will be informative to consider further the great variety of information which pervades our everyday lives, and with which an information service may have to deal.

If we consider a medium-sized organization, such as a small manufacturer or retailer, we can see that there are many distinct, though sometimes overlapping, flows of information through the organization. There will be information relating to the organization's 'core activities' – production figures, sales targets – and to the 'public face' of the organization – advertising and publicity, annual reports, mission statements. The human resources department will gather and use information related to staff, there will be minutes of board meetings, financial records relating to transactions, internal memos, e-mails with record status, tenders and contracts, press releases, utilities bills, leases and bank statements.

Another example of a medium-sized organization, a university, would create and maintain, in addition to most of the above, records relating to students and their achievements, research data, information relating to student unions, clubs, societies and accommodation, a library or libraries, archives and a whole range of publications.

Neither of these lists is intended to be complete, but rather to be indicative of the range of roles which information may play inside an organization. Some data will be used in more than one context – for example, a student's name and address might appear on an e-mail enquiring about admission, on their personal file, on their marks transcript, on a student loan application, in the membership records of a society, and so on. We will see, later, that this re-use of data in different contexts can lead to efficiency, but can also be the cause of troublesome errors. Chapter 3 is concerned primarily with *data quality* – what it is and how we can maintain, and even enhance it, to add value to it as a vital component in business processes.

Where is our information?

So, how does something as intangible as information, the very definition of which is open to interpretation, come to be regarded as an asset? It is not obvious where it might appear on an accountant's balance sheet. How could a value be put on it? How could it be realized, or converted into cash? It may cost money to acquire data, and to process the data into information, but that does not guarantee that the information has a value. If it can be sold, or if it can be used, we can put a value on it. We can even identify a kind of 'negative value' – information which is worthless to the holder, but which has a cost associated with its loss, and this apparent contradiction will be discussed in Chapter 2.

Part of the difficulty in seeing information as having value is probably due to its intangible nature – it seems as if the more we hear about 'information overload', the less able we are to perceive its cause. Information storage media have become more compact, although many 'legacy' formats are still with us, and their presence may in itself be problematic – paper files take up a lot of space compared to CDs, for example. However, as the physical 'footprint' of information storage decreases, from paper files to magnetic tape reels and cassettes, through 8-inch floppy discs to 5.25-inch and 3.5-inch, then to CDs and to USB sticks, and now off into 'the cloud', our ability to keep track of the information the media contain appears to decrease proportionately. Since the storage capability of the media has increased vastly, compared to the rate at which their size has reduced, this means that we are behaving much less responsibly, with much more information, than ever before.

The move of huge amounts of data to 'the cloud' may be as far as we can go in this direction – individuals, and organizations are now storing their data on the internet in places unknown to them, on servers they do not own, and often with little grasp of the issues and implications of their decision to do so. Perhaps this is information at its most abstract, at least for the current generation of computing – effectively omnipresent, but attached to no identifiable substrate.

Threats

The 'omnipresence' of data and information introduces still more problems, because it introduces more previously unknown factors to our dealings with information. When information is available from anywhere there is a network connection (which, of course, need no longer be a physical connection, thanks to the advent of Wi-Fi, GPS, etc.) then we may access it via mobile devices such as laptops, tablets and smartphones. This, however, presents another security challenge, because mobile devices can store data, and can retain the protocols – usernames and passwords – required to access data remotely. Chapter 4 will deal with threats to our information security.

Standards, frameworks and a framework for information governance and assurance

Chapter 5 looks at international standards concerned with how these security issues may be addressed, and at other standards related to risk management and to business continuity management. We see that these topics are concerned with the organization's interactions with its environment, and note that information management is an important factor in all of them. In Chapter 6 we note that, in general, standards recommend the adoption of a 'framework', which can then be implemented as actual practices within an organization. We examine the 'framework' concept and suggest a model for a 'meta-framework' for information governance and assurance, whereby the other frameworks can be given a place in an overall scheme which can be adopted by an organization at a strategic level.

Policy

These issues, amongst others which we will deal with in the course of this book, have led to a perceived need for 'information governance'. The term can be understood in (at least) two senses, the more commonly used being that of external regulations imposed upon those who work with information – the mechanisms of 'governing' information-handling organizations. However, we will also be using the term in another sense – the measures which an organization can, and ought to, put in place, in order that its handling of information is conducted in such a way as to maximize benefits to the organization. The idea here is not one of simple compliance with strictures imposed from outside, but rather one of actively seeking the means whereby information policy can enhance the operations of the organization.

A major theme throughout this book will be the desirability of developing a comprehensive information policy for the information service. Each of Chapters 2–5 will address specific areas of the overall policy which relate to the chapter topic.

Assurance

Another repeated theme which can usefully be introduced here is that of 'assurance'. In the sense in which it is used in this book, 'assurance' implies confidence – confidence that you as an as organization have 'done the right thing' by your use of information, confidence that you have applied standards where appropriate and confidence that your organization is compliant with any applicable legislation. It also means that other organizations with whom you may have a business partnership can deal with you in confidence, and that potential customers can be assured of the high standards and stability of your organization.

How to use this book

The assumption will be made that the reader is interested in these topics from the perspective of the information service, so sometimes second person ('you should . . .') will be used, rather than repeating the more stilted ('the organization should . . .') construction. Each of the following chapters includes at the end some small exercises or points for discussion related to its content. Some of these involve finding out about your own organization, if you work in one, or your institution, if you are a student, and the answers will be different for every reader. They could be used as points for discussion in a seminar, or as a starting point for background research to begin your own information governance project. However, where there are more obvious answers, these will be discussed briefly in an appendix at the end of the book.

CHAPTER 2

The laws and regulations

Introduction

In this chapter, we will examine the external drivers which influence organizations towards practising good information governance. These are pieces of legislation, regulation and standards which are imposed from outside the organization, and which either must be complied with in order to avoid penalties, or which define benchmarks against which the practices and performance of the organization can be judged.

Sometimes these, in particular the pieces of legislation, are themselves referred to as 'information governance', in that they impose rules which govern what organizations do with information. However, as we've seen in Chapter 1, a more constructive way of understanding the term is to think of 'information governance' as those practices which lead to efficient, effective and ethical use of information. The fact that we also avoid legal repercussions simply means that the law recognizes our practices as being correct.

The specific laws and regulations dealt with in this chapter will be those which apply in the UK, as space does not permit discussion of equivalent legislation in other legislatures, but it will be found that similar legislation exists in a large number of countries – in March 2013, Rwanda became the 94th country to pass a Right to Information Act (Freedominfo.org, 2013). The equivalence of EC countries' data protection laws to those in the UK is discussed in the section 'The eighth principle' (page 32), as is the list of 'third' countries recognized by the EC as having equivalent legislation. Other states, including the 21 members of the Asia-Pacific Economic Co-operation Group (APEC) have agreed on privacy principles, and Argentina, Canada, Hong Kong, Israel and Russia have based their laws on the European model (Kuner, 2010).

The USA has had a Freedom of Information Act since 1966. It applies to records held by federal agencies, such as the Department of Justice and the Department of Health and Human Services, and gives individuals the right to access any agency record, except for those protected from public disclosure for reasons of national security, for example. It also requires the agencies to automatically publish other information, including lists of frequently asked questions and answers to them (FAQs). It is the responsibility of the enquirers to determine which agency has the records they require, but all agencies have a website which lists the types of records they hold. This stance of actively making records available is endorsed as good policy by the UK Information Commissioner's Office, and we shall discuss later why it is a part of a well thought-out information governance policy.

We can see from Figure 2.1 that all requests relating to data which we publish, or are advised to publish, will be answered, but that there are some requests in the areas of personal data, sensitive personal data, environmental data and other data where exemptions may apply which relieve us of the obligation to answer.

These laws and regulations are expressions of a relatively new and 'open' attitude to information – that people have the right to know about the activities of, and information held by, public authorities; that giving the public access to, for example, environmental information increases public engagement with environmental issues, making public bodies more accountable, and increasing public trust in them.

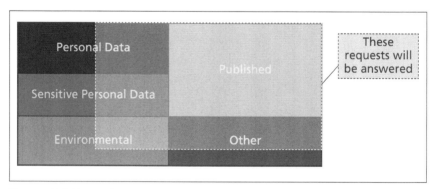

Figure 2.1 For various reasons, some requests will be exempted from being answered

A standard for records

In much of the rest of this book, we'll be discussing records, and what may and may not, what ought and ought not to, be done with them. '[R]ecords are recorded information. Indeed, a record may be defined as *any information captured in reproducible form that is required for conducting business*' (Penn, Pennix and Coulson, 1994, 3). As the authors observe, there are different definitions of 'information', depending on whether you believe it is raw data, whether it has metadata added, or is data which have been transformed into 'knowledge', but the important point is that we need systems for handling it, in order that it may be used in 'conducting business' – another expression open to a wide range of interpretation.

As you might expect, there is a lot of recorded information in a university, for example, but not all of it is in the form of records. There is a great deal of recorded information in the library, but, aside from some archival material, which is in the form of records, the library stock is not used, or required, for conducting business. Of course, the library could not operate without stock, and the university could not operate without the library, but the information in the library stock is not required for conducting business. We could exchange one library book on records management for another without any major disruption, but if we transposed personnel records, or student transcripts, or salary records, it does not take much imagination to see the trouble that might result.

Records have been kept for thousands of years, the media changing from clay tablets to papyrus, from paper to electronic and optical media, but the idea of records management as a function central to the operation of an organization is of relatively recent origin. Until the period following World War 2, the 'records management' function tended to concentrate on amassing material – the 'keep everything' strategy. Whilst this might suffice for limited numbers of records, we have all heard of the 'information explosion', and mere accumulation does not enhance usability. There is no value in keeping everything if you cannot find the item you want, when you want it.

Organizations are under more pressure than ever before to be efficient, and there are also legal requirements to demonstrate efficient and effective records management – the Data Protection Act 1998 and the Freedom of Information Act 2000 are two of the legal instruments enforcing these standards in the UK – but there are equivalent pieces of legislation in many other jurisdictions, and the increase in online activity means that we all have an interest in ensuring that our personal information is safe from abuse, and that we have access to the information which organizations hold about us.

So, there is a competitive advantage to be gained from effective records management, and there is also a requirement to be able to demonstrate good practice in how it is carried out.

The record life-cycle

One of the post-World War 2 innovations in records management was the notion that records have a life-cycle – they pass through different stages and types of use, beginning with their creation, moving through a period of active use, then into a semi-active period, and finally to the stage of archiving or disposal. This is also reflected in the ways in which records are managed physically – active records will most likely be found close to those who work with them, perhaps in in- and out-trays on people's desks, perhaps in filing cabinets. Semi-active records will probably be in files, and inactive records will either be disposed of or may be moved to off-site storage, should they have archival value. Electronic records will undergo a similar process – from 'live' files to archives, perhaps written to optical disks, perhaps deleted.

Costs and benefits

Records, particularly paper records, are a source of cost, relating to their creation, handling, and storage. One of the benefits of a good records management policy is that significant savings can be made in the office space which has been used to store records which need not be there. This can be a major selling point in convincing management of the need for a records management programme, but the fact is that there are many other drivers, which are not so easily measured as the cost per square metre of housing filing cabinets, or the cost per gigabyte of computer disk storage.

The benefits are partly from the absence of things that *don't* happen if you have a good records management policy. Your organization is able to face an audit with confidence, because invoices and receipts are properly managed. A Freedom of Information request can be handled with ease, because the relevant records are easily traceable. Employees can feel secure that their personal data are handled correctly. Customers can feel secure that their contact and credit card details are not abused. Even the author of a corporate history can trace documents of historical value, in the archives.

Desirable qualities of records

In order to be authoritative, records ought to possess certain qualities, usually expressed as reliability, authenticity, integrity and usability. Briefly, these can be summarized thus:

1 **Reliability** means that the record can be trusted as a full and accurate representation of the activity that it records.
2 **Authenticity** means that the record is what it appears to be – that it has been created by authorized and identifiable individuals and processes. Policies and processes should be identified and recorded, to ensure that records are protected from unauthorized addition, deletion and alteration.
3 **Integrity** refers to records being complete, and free from unauthorized alteration. Audit trails should be in place to demonstrate this. Integrity may also refer to the structural integrity of the physical and logical relationships amongst the content-related elements of a website. If the structural of a website is impaired, its reliability and authenticity might be affected.
4 **Usability** means that records ought to be available and complete, so filing systems should be clear and unambiguous, and latest, authoritative versions of records should be easy to find and use.
(US National Archives and Records Administration, 2005)

A standard for records management

Almost all organizations must handle records, and there has been a good deal of material written on the topic. There is also an international standard, ISO 15489: Information and Documentation – Records Management (ISO/IEC, 2001a; ISO/IEC, 2001b), which provides advice on records management and the creation of a framework for a records management workflow. This is the first of several international standards we shall be discussing in the book and, like the others, it has a dual significance for the organizations which use it. First, it describes best practice. Second, adherence to the standards, which in the case of some standards can be certified by appropriate authorities, is a badge of good practice which the world at large can understand.

ISO 15489 is in two parts, the first constituting a general briefing, for all staff and management, on a framework for best practice in records management, and the second going into greater detail about designing and implementing a framework for records systems. BSI Standards publish three books entitled *Effective Records Management* that give practical advice on using the standard (Best, 2002; McLeod, 2002; Jones, 2003).

The standard sets out the characteristics of records and systems, which we've covered briefly above, and principles for managing records – what records ought to be created, how to organize them and comply with legal policies, organizational needs and relevant standards. It also discusses the instruments required, such as a classification scheme and a controlled vocabulary, and how to document a retention schedule, describing what records ought to be kept, for how long and why, and recording the reasons for doing so. Finally, it describes records management processes:

- capture
- registration
- classification
- access and security classification
- identification of disposition status
- storage
- use and tracking
- implementation of disposition.

The standard has been adopted, or practices based on it have been adopted and recommended, by the National Archive of Australia, the UK National Archive (TNA), the US National Archives and Records Administration (NARA), numerous UK county councils and universities worldwide (Higgins, 2007).

The Information Commissioner's Office

The UK Information Commissioner's Office (ICO) is 'The UK's independent authority set up to *uphold information rights in the public interest*, [emphasis in original] promoting openness by public bodies, [such as schools and the Health Service] and data privacy for individuals' (Information Commissioner's Office, 2012a). As the quote suggests, the ICO has responsibility for providing advice on a range of legislation and regulation. In addition to those discussed in this chapter, it covers the Privacy and Electronic Communications (EC Directive) Regulations 2003, which cover such matters as nuisance telephone calls and 'spam' e-mails, and the INSPIRE regulations, which oblige UK public authorities to release information about spatial data sets. The ICO publicizes the legislation, produces guides to compliance, maintains a register of data controllers, carries out audits, deals with complaints and monitors compliance. It has powers of enforcement – it can currently issue monetary penalties of up to £500,000 (Information Commissioner's Office, 2013a), can issue enforcement notices and can bring criminal prosecutions. Its website (http://ico.gov.uk) is the definitive source of information and advice on these matters.

The reference to an EC Directive in the Privacy and Electronic Communications (EC Directive) Regulations 2003 is because of the way that European Community legislation works. The EC issues Directives which set out goals. All member countries, or those specified in the Directives, are bound to implement laws which meet these goals within a certain specified period. How the law is implemented is at the discretion of the member state, because they may have different existing legislation, and so need different adjustments to bring that into line with EC Directives. Under the European Communities Act 1972, which is a piece of UK legislation, the UK parliament can implement, by means of Regulations, changes which need to be made to UK law. This gives a certain common purpose to the laws of EC member communities, which we shall also see expressed in the Environmental Information Regulations, described later in this chapter.

The Freedom of Information Act 2000

The UK Freedom of Information Act 2000 (FOIA) applies to 'public bodies' as defined in the Act. In broad terms, this means: government and local government departments and legislative bodies; the armed forces and the police; the National Health Service; maintained schools and institutions of further and higher education; and other public bodies. The last category includes a list of around 400 non-departmental public bodies such as The National Archives, the Bank of England and public broadcasting authorities.

The Secretary of State can add to the list bodies which appear to be 'providing functions of a public nature' (Information Commissioner's Office, 2012a) or acting for public authorities under contract. The Secretary can also remove organizations from the list if they appear no longer to be acting in this way. The list also includes publicly owned companies, companies wholly owned by the Crown, and companies owned by public authorities. Consequently, a very wide range of organizations are subject to the Act, which was introduced following a 1997 White Paper stating the government's intention to promote openness and trust, and to reduce unnecessary secrecy. The Act covers any recorded information, and requests can be made by anybody – they do not have to be UK citizens or residents. The FOIA applies in England, Wales and Northern Ireland – Scotland has separate, though similar, legislation, the Freedom of Information (Scotland) Act 2002 (FOISA), and its own Information Commissioner.

Requirements of the FOIA

There are two types of requirement under the FOIA. One concerns the publication of information by public authorities. These are required to publish information – every public authority must have a publication scheme approved by the ICO, and the ICO makes available a model scheme (Information Commissioner's Office, 2013b) on which individual authorities' schemes must be based. Material to be published and made available under this scheme includes information about what the authority does, how it spends its budget, its decisions, policies and procedures, the services it offers, and lists and registers it holds that relate to its functions. It must also publish methods by which the information will be made available (for example, some types of planning may have to be viewed by visiting a display), and charges applicable to obtaining the information (for example, the costs of photocopying or postage). As implied by these examples, the information does not have to be published on a website, although many authorities will find that a website is the most convenient way of publishing much of it.

The second type of information is that which might be requested by a member of the public, organizations, such as the press, and indeed other public authorities (although the ICO observes that such information needs can normally be handled through other channels). This covers all information other than that covered by the publication scheme.

What must actually be supplied is the information contained in documents. Note that e-mails are regarded as being documents, but only those stored in an organization's system, not those in personal e-mail accounts of employees. You are not expected to supply information that exists only in the sense that someone knows it, nor are you expected to combine existing information to answer questions, although doing so if the work involved is not excessive would constitute good practice. You are not expected to disclose information which is still in preparation for publication. You do not have to disclose information held on behalf of another organization.

Freedom of Information requests

The mechanism for requesting the information is a Freedom of Information request, which to be valid must be in writing, include the requestor's real name and a contact address, and describe the information required. Not every request for information will be an FOI request, and not every request should be treated as such. However, requests identifying themselves as FOI requests and fulfilling the criteria for validity must be so treated. Requests which do not satisfy the criteria, or are not framed as FOI requests, should still be dealt with where possible, as a matter of simple helpfulness, and many requests will not in any case relate to recorded information, or can be dealt with easily by reference to the publication scheme, discussed above.

If the request is for personal information, it should be dealt with under the terms of the Data Protection Act, as a Subject Access request, and if it is for environmental information, it falls under the Environmental Information Regulations. Both these cases will be covered later in this chapter.

Time for compliance

If the request does not fall into any of these categories, it should be dealt with under the FOI, meaning that within 20 working days from the day following receipt of the request, the organization must make a written response. If requests are ambiguous, or if it is unclear what information is being requested, the organization must contact the requestor and seek clarification, and the time within which it must comply begins once the clarification has been received. Once the information is identified, the organization must confirm whether or not they have it, and must provide it, if they do. There are circumstances under which the organization may refuse to provide some or all of the existing information requested, but it would normally still be expected to confirm the existence of the information, or of further information, if all of the information has not been provided. There are, however, instances where the organization may refuse to provide all or some of the existing information requested, or may decline to confirm or deny the existence of the information. For example, if a public authority was asked about plans to inspect an organization, to confirm or deny the existence of such plans would give the organization the chance to prepare for inspection, and so give it an unfair advantage. In this case the authority has grounds under section 30 of the Act neither to confirm nor deny the existence of such information. The relevant exemption must be cited in the refusal, unless to do so would in itself confirm or deny the existence of the information, and the decision to apply this exemption from disclosure must, as always, be taken in the public interest (Ministry of Justice, 2012a).

Format of information supplied

The requestor can state in the request how they want the information to be supplied, but the ICO advises that in the absence of such specification, any reasonable format will suffice. Costs may be charged for printing, photocopying and postage in this respect.

When an organization may refuse an FOI request

A request may be refused on the grounds that providing the

information would be too expensive in terms of monetary cost or the cost in staff time, if the request is 'vexatious' or if it repeats a previous request from the same requestor. 'Currently, the cost limit for complying with a request or a linked series of requests from the same person or group is set at £600 for central government, Parliament and the Armed Forces, and £450 for all other public authorities' (Information Commissioner's Office, 2013c). It may be that the information is already available, or that it is in preparation for publication. There are also exemptions based on the nature of the information requested, for example, if its disclosure could result in harm to a person or if damage to an organization's commercial interests might arise from its disclosure. There are exemptions for personal information covered by the Data Protection Act, and there are 'absolute' exemptions relating to defence, security and international relations, for example. In cases where exemptions are not absolute, the organization is required to decide whether disclosure would be harmful or against the public interest – that is whether the public interest would be done a greater disservice by not supplying the information than by supplying it.

Publication scheme

As stated under 'Requirements of the FOIA' (see page 16), the other aspect of the FOIA is the publication scheme. Essentially, what this does is to pre-emptively make information available – you can respond to enquirers that the information is on your website, thus appearing to have anticipated their request, and reducing the time pressure of an FOI request; you are ensuring that the information they find is what you intend to be found, so that it is not assembled under time pressure from other sources and presented in a less carefully considered format; you have effectively 'answered the question already' – since there is already a 'public-facing' answer to the enquiry, there is no perceived need for the enquirer to persist in their enquiry. We have transparency, openness, accountability, and the USA (which, as we saw in the Introduction to this chapter, has its own, similar, legislation) sees it as opening up the democratic process to inspection. Saying that the information is available on your website is an acceptable, and even quite helpful, response to an FOI request, and the question should really be, why would you not adopt a policy of publication? It should serve to forestall the vexatious or time-wasting enquirer. Should an enquirer persist beyond the published information, however, there is a definite need for a robust and defensible records management policy.

Data protection

As stated in the previous section, one of the grounds on which a public sector organization may refuse to disclose information is that it is personal information covered by the Data Protection Act, so the next step in examining an organization's obligations is to look at what that means.

The Data Protection Act 1998 (DPA) is more widely applicable than the FOIA. Whereas the FOIA applies only to the public sector, the DPA applies to anyone handling personal data about individuals.

Data subject to the DPA
Definitions of data

The Act's definition of 'personal data' is quite complex. 'Data' are considered to be any of the following:

- information which is being processed by computer, or is recorded so that it can be so processed
- information that is part of a 'relevant filing system', or is recorded so that it can be part of one
- part of an 'accessible record', which does not come into these categories but falls under section 68 of the Act
- recorded information which does not fall into any of those categories, but is held by a public authority.

These definitions cover computing systems and their storage media, filing systems from which information concerning an individual can be easily retrieved, and data which have been prepared for input to either of these types of system (for example, recorded on data input sheets, prior to actual input). The reference to section 68 concerns rights of access that existed prior to the DPA, to data that were not held on systems like computers and the 'relevant filing systems' referred to above. In order to preserve those rights, after the introduction of the DPA, they are listed in section 68 of the Act, and refer to individuals' health records, individuals' educational records and 'accessible' records held by local authorities concerning housing or social services.

Personal data

The next step in the definition brings us to 'personal data'. These are considered to be:

> data which relate to a living individual who can be identified – (a) from those data, or (b) from those data and other information which is in the possession of, or is likely to come into the possession of, the data controller, and includes any expression of opinion about the individual and any indication of the intentions of the data controller or any other person in respect of the individual.
>
> Information Commissioner's Office (2013d)

The ICO notes that there are two important points about this definition. First, if the data held can be put together with other data, for example a key file identifying the anonymized interviewees of a research report, and used to identify individuals, then the interviews are personal data. The other is that opinions of, and declarations of intentions towards, individuals are personal data about those individuals. Examples here might be an e-mail between managers expressing an opinion of an employee, or declaring an intention to influence the outcome of someone's interview for a post.

Sensitive personal data

Finally, 'sensitive personal data' are personal data relating to an individual's:

- racial or ethnic origin
- political opinions
- religious or similar beliefs
- membership of a trade union
- physical or mental condition

- sex life
- status as an offender or alleged offender
- involvement in proceedings for an offence or alleged offence.

There is a clear inference to be made from this list that the 'sensitivity' of the data results from the possibility of their being used to discriminate about the individual, and since they are data concerning facts which might not otherwise be obvious to those who do not have access to the data, they receive special treatment under the Act.

Requirements of the DPA

The DPA sets out requirements for the processing of personal data, and more stringent requirements for the processing of sensitive personal data:

> Processing, in relation to information or data, means obtaining, recording or holding the information or data or carrying out any operation or set of operations on the information or data, including –
>
> a) organisation, adaptation or alteration of the information or data,
> b) retrieval, consultation or use of the information or data,
> c) disclosure of the information or data by transmission, dissemination or otherwise making available, or
> d) alignment, combination, blocking, erasure or destruction of the information or data.
>
> Information Commissioner's Office (2013d)

Data subjects, controllers and processors

More definitions now. The simplest is **data subject** – the person that the personal data are about. A **data controller** is a person or organization who has responsibility for the data – who decides the reason for which the data are being processed, and the manner in which it is processed. A **data processor** is a person or organization who, or which, processes data on behalf of a data controller. This might be as a result of an outsourcing agreement, for example where a call centre acts on behalf of another organization, using data about that organization's customers.

The responsibility for processing the data in compliance with the Act still rests with the data controller, though. Every data controller, unless exempt, must register with the ICO. Exemptions are available to not-for-profit organizations, those who use personal data for very restricted purposes and with the agreement of the data subjects, and personal address lists held by individuals; the ICO publishes a self-test (Information Commissioner's Office, 2013e).

DPA principles

These are the eight principles listed in Schedule 1 of the DPA:

1. Personal data shall be processed fairly and lawfully and, in particular, shall not be processed unless –
   (a) at least one of the conditions in Schedule 2 is met, and
   (b) in the case of sensitive personal data, at least one of the conditions in Schedule 3 is also met.
2. Personal data shall be obtained only for one or more specified and lawful purposes, and shall not be further processed in any manner incompatible with that purpose or those purposes.
3. Personal data shall be adequate, relevant and not excessive in relation to the purpose or purposes for which they are processed.
4. Personal data shall be accurate and, where necessary, kept up to date.
5. Personal data processed for any purpose or purposes shall not be kept for longer than is necessary for that purpose or those purposes.
6. Personal data shall be processed in accordance with the rights of data subjects under this Act.
7. Appropriate technical and organisational measures shall be taken against unauthorised or unlawful processing of personal data and against accidental loss or destruction of, or damage to, personal data.
8. Personal data shall not be transferred to a country or territory outside the European Economic Area unless that country or territory ensures an adequate level of protection for the rights and freedoms of data subjects in relation to the processing of personal data.

Data Protection Act 1998

The first principle – conditions

As is often the case with legal documents, the language in the DPA is expressed so as to reduce ambiguity, rather than to make for easy reading. Although the principles are not in themselves particularly convoluted, they are followed in the Act by a section on their interpretation which is less easy to understand. The ICO also offers its own interpretation, and makes the point that in Principle 1, since the conditions which must be met in order for data to be processed are in addition to the requirement that the purpose for which they are being processed is 'fair and lawful', it is advisable to consider fairness and legality first. Just because the conditions are met, in other words, that does not ensure the fairness and lawfulness of what is being done.

The conditions themselves are in two sets, one of which relates to personal data, followed by a more restrictive set which relates to sensitive personal data – Schedules 2 and 3, respectively. In each case, at least one of the conditions in the applicable Schedule must be met.

Schedule 2 conditions

The first, and less restrictive, set of conditions are that the data subject, the person the data is about, has given his or her consent that the data be processed, or that the processing is 'necessary' for one of a number of reasons, which could be:

1 The performance of a contract to which the data subject is a party, or in order that a contract may be entered into.
2 A legal obligation other than a contract on the data processor.
3 A need to protect the data subject's 'vital interests' – quite literally; according to the ICO, this applies only to 'cases of life or death', for example, where disclosure of medical information could help in an accident victim's treatment.
4 Administration of justice, or the carrying out of 'statutory, governmental, or other public functions'. This is a condition which covers those bodies responsible for such functions, so that, for example, a police force or a government department, in the process of carrying out its functions, may process personal data without the data subject having given consent.

Finally, there is a 'legitimate interests' condition, which has three requirements. First, the processing must be necessary for the data controller's legitimate interests, or for those of a third party to whom they want to disclose the information. The ICO gives the example of a finance house disclosing the details of a defaulting customer to a debt-collecting agency (Information Commissioner's Office, 2013f).

The second requirement, once the first requirement is met, is that the interests of the data controller and the data subject must both be considered. If the processing has unwarranted repercussions on the rights, freedoms or legitimate interests of the data subject, then the processing does not meet the requirement. The key word here is 'unwarranted' – although in the debt collection example, the two parties might disagree about the action, the finance company has a reasonable right to try to recover its money.

Last, the data processing under this condition must be fair, lawful and in keeping with the provisions of the DPA.

Schedule 3 conditions

When processing sensitive personal data, in addition to at least one of the Schedule 2 conditions being met, at least one of the Schedule 3 conditions must be met. These are:

1 That the individual has given explicit consent, where 'explicit' would be taken to mean consent to processing those particular, sensitive, data, and not just the more general personal data already considered.
2 Where the processing has to take place so that the processor can comply with employment law.
3 Where the data subject's 'vital interests' are at stake, but the data subject's consent has not been obtained, or cannot be obtained, or where another individual's vital interests are at stake, but 'the individual's consent has been unreasonably withheld.' This last one needs some untangling.
4 That the data processing is done by a not-for-profit organization, and does not involve disclosure of the data to a third party, unless with the individual's consent.
5 That the individual has him/herself made the information public.

Here we might think of people whose otherwise 'sensitive' information regarding their trade union membership or political affiliation is made known by them wearing badges, or publicly exhibiting political posters.

6 If the processing is necessary in relation to legal proceedings.
7 If the processing is necessary for 'administering justice', and other public functions – essentially the same condition as the fourth reason in the Schedule 2 framework as set out above.
8 If the processing is necessary for medical purposes, and is carried out either by a health professional or by somebody under the same duty of professional confidentiality.
9 If it is necessary that the processing is done in order to monitor equality of opportunity, and with safeguards for individuals' rights. An example here might be if sensitive data about ethnic origin were collected by an employer.

'Necessary' in the last four conditions has quite a strict interpretation, meaning that there is no other reasonable way that the results referred to in each case could be achieved, and necessity cannot be simply due to the way the data processor chooses to operate.

Extensions to the Schedule 3 conditions

There are two Statutory Instruments which extend the scope of the Schedule 3 conditions:

1 Statutory Instrument 2000 No. 417: The Data Protection (Processing of Sensitive Personal Data) Order 2000
2 Statutory Instrument 2002 No. 2905: The Data Protection (Processing of Sensitive Personal Data) (Elected Representatives) Order 2002.

These additionally provide for the processing of sensitive personal data, by, on behalf of, or for disclosure to, an 'elected representative' (a Member of Parliament, of National Assemblies, or of a local authority):

- in order to prevent or detect any unlawful act
- in order to protect the public against dishonesty or malpractice

- to be published in the public interest
- in order to provide confidential counselling, advice or any other service
- for carrying out of insurance business
- for monitoring equal opportunity regarding beliefs or mental health
- by registered political parties for legitimate political activities
- when it is necessary for research purposes
- when the processing 'is necessary for the exercise of any functions conferred on a constable by any rule of law.'

    The Data Protection (Processing of Sensitive Personal Data) Order 2000

Remember that all this is just in order to comply with the first of the eight principles. The data have to be processed fairly and lawfully, and at least one of the appropriate set of conditions has to be met. The ICO points out that overall fairness should be a more important consideration than obtaining consent, which, although listed first in each schedule, is, in each schedule, only one of many equally valid conditions.

The second principle

Now that we have established whether processing can take place at all, the second principle begins to examine how the processing must be done, and begins with the reason for which the data is obtained. 'Obtaining' may not appear to be 'processing', but remember that 'processing' encompasses many operations relating to the data. The second principle says that the data must only be obtained for 'specified and lawful purposes', and that they must not be 'further processed' in a manner 'incompatible' with those purposes. In other words, before you collect personal data, you must have a justification for doing so, and that purpose is the only thing you are allowed to use the data for – if you want to use them for something else as well, that requires separate justification, perhaps a different agreement with the data subject and perhaps a separate notification to the ICO.

As an example, suppose an organization collects employees' personal data for human resources (HR) and payroll purposes, and is registered with the ICO as a data controller in those respects. If a member of the public telephones, asking for contact details of an employee, who is an old friend of theirs, the organization should not disclose the information, because that is not the purpose for which the data were collected. Disclosure is 'processing', and although the employee will have given consent to supply the data, and keeping the data for HR and payroll is necessary for the organization's legitimate interests, it is unlikely that the employee has consented to allow their personal data to be disclosed to all.

Another example occurs quite frequently in universities – after assessments, there is a phone call from a student's parent, or someone purporting to be a student's parent, asking for their mark in the assessment. Disclosure to this person is not the reason why records of student marks are kept, and apart from the question of identity (a telephone call would not be sufficient to identify even the student), the marks should not be disclosed.

The third, fourth and fifth principles

These can be considered as a group – as the ICO notes (Information Commissioner's Office, 2012b), they are all related to data standards, a topic to which we shall be returning in Chapter 5, but which is probably easier to grasp in this scenario of very well defined, and relatively simple, data.

The principles stipulate, respectively, that personal data should be:

- adequate, relevant and not excessive in relation to the purposes for which they are processed
- accurate and, where necessary, kept up to date, and
- kept for no longer than is necessary for the purpose, or purposes, for which they have been processed.

Data Protection Act 1998

The standards are interrelated because relevance and accuracy are closely connected, as are being kept up to date and for no longer than is necessary, which could also be considered excessive, and so on. The Act splits the requirements down like this for clarity of definition, but, in practice, the data controller will want to consider them together, or at least be always conscious of the linkages amongst them.

The third principle

The third principle is about the amount of data that are held – enough to serve the purpose for which they are processed, but no more than that, remembering that 'processing' includes storage. For example, a conscientious firm that installs replacement windows might build up a bank of information about the properties and owners of houses in an area, and approach them with a view to selling them new windows. This might be done by telephoning the properties, and asking about ownership/tenancy, number of rooms, number of windows, and so on. It would be appropriate for the organization to retain more detailed information about the owners and properties where interest is expressed in the product, but only sufficient information about the others to ensure that they are not approached again.

A social club planning a group holiday would probably collect next-of-kin contact details for those going on the holiday, but it could be considered irrelevant and excessive to do so for all members – information should not be kept just in case it might be useful in future.

The fourth principle

Accuracy and currency of information appear quite simple concepts, but some questions of interpretation can arise. Not all information can be checked, but the data controller should take reasonable steps to do so, and ensure that the source of personal data is known and recorded. If the accuracy of data is challenged, the challenge and the need to update the data should be considered. At a fairly mundane level, and far predating the DPA, this is one of the reasons why the minutes of meetings are read and approved by the next in a series of meetings, so that an accurate record of the proceedings is kept. There may be cases where personal data should be kept about something which is not true, in a sense. For example, if disciplinary proceedings are taken against an employee, who is found not to have breached the relevant regulations, then the employee should not be recorded as having breached the regulations, which seems quite obvious. However, if the employee requests that reference to the proceedings be removed from the records, there are good reasons for refusing to do so, because that record is accurate.

The social club from a previous example may hold records of names and addresses of lapsed members for accounting or archival purposes, but is not obliged to update these records with subsequent changes of address, although this would be the case with current members. If information is held for certain purposes, such as historical research, then the fact of updating it might invalidate those purposes. The information should be accurate with respect to the period it reflects, and this should be recorded.

The fifth principle

Just as these three principles, three, four and five, can be seen as an introduction to data quality, principle five in itself introduces the idea of the **record retention schedule**, a central component in the Records Management toolkit. The principle itself is stated simply: 'Personal data processed for any purpose or purposes shall not be kept for longer than is necessary for that purpose or those purposes' (Data Protection Act 1998). However, as the ICO points out, in practice this implies reviewing why you keep the personal data, how long you need to keep them for, and ensuring that they are disposed of securely when they are no longer needed. The ICO adds that information which is out of date should be updated, archived or securely deleted. This last requirement is not immediately obvious from the statement of the fifth principle alone, but is implicit in reading it in conjunction with principles three and four – if you keep the data, they must be accurate. If they are to be accurate, that means they must be updated when necessary. If they are being kept for historical purposes, they must be archived, so that they are no longer regarded as current. If none of these apply, they are no longer necessary, so must be deleted, and this must be done securely, so that there is no danger of them being mistaken for current data, or otherwise misused. Since an organization may be keeping many types of information, for many purposes, it will probably be desirable to formalize the procedures involved in dealing with information into a records retention schedule. All records should be reviewed regularly for accuracy and currency, but for certain classes (or series, to use the records management term) of records, decisions can be made in advance, as a matter of policy, which decide their eventual disposal, whether disposal to an archive or to a secure method of deletion, and the timing of this disposal. Often, this will be a matter of organizational policy (for example, an organization might store customer sales transaction records for three years, in case of returns or guarantee claims) or of legal or professional requirement (the educational records of a midwife might be retained for as long as she continues in practice). The reason for the decision should be recorded in the schedule, alongside the record series and the decision itself. In many cases, where records are stored electronically, the process can be semi-automated (subject to human confirmation and override, in the event of anomalies).

The sixth principle

The sixth principle is that data shall be processed in accordance with the rights of individuals under the Act, and there are six of these. An individual has:

- a right of access to his or her personal data
- a right to object to processing that is likely to cause or is causing damage or distress
- a right to prevent processing for direct marketing
- a right to object to decisions being taken by automated means
- a right in certain circumstances to have inaccurate personal data rectified, blocked, erased or destroyed
- a right to claim compensation for damages caused by a breach of the Act.

Information Commissioner's Office (2013g)

The first of these rights is expressed through a Subject Access Request (SAR), the individual's mechanism under the Act for finding out what personal data regarding them is being processed. The SAR is a very important topic in practice, and will be discussed following this discussion of the principles. The others are rights to modification of either the data or the processing, and are explained in detail by the ICO (Information Commissioner's Office, 2013g).

The seventh principle

The seventh principle is 'Appropriate technical and organisational measures shall be taken against unauthorised or unlawful processing of personal data and against accidental loss or destruction of, or damage to, personal data' (Data Protection Act 1998). Chapters 4 and 5 of this book will deal with security measures regarding this, and other, information.

The eighth principle

The final principle concerns the sending of data outside the European Economic Area (EEA), and can be summarized as stipulating that personal data must not be sent outside the EEA, unless to a jurisdiction (country or territory) which provides at least the same level of rights and freedoms to individuals regarding their personal data as they have within the EEA. Remember from the previous discussion that the structure of EC directives and local implementations guarantees that all EC member countries will have legislation with equivalent impact, although this situation may have been reached by different routes in different countries. The EEA countries are the 27 EU member countries, plus Norway, Lichtenstein and Iceland, and the EC maintains and publishes a list of other countries, or 'third countries', which it recognizes as 'providing adequate protection' (European Commission, 2013).

The list includes the 'Safe Harbor' scheme, under which US companies may voluntarily sign up to abide by seven principles of data processing, and render themselves accountable to the Federal Trade Commission or other oversight schemes for doing so. The scheme is explained on the US Department of Commerce website (Export.gov, 2012).

The final entry on the list is 'the transfer of Air Passenger Name Record to the United States Bureau of Customs and Border Protection'. This concerns a 2007 agreement that the US authority would regulate and adequately protect such data supplied by EU airlines. The data is required by the US authorities for security purposes, but, because the US is not a 'third country', and the US Department of Homeland Security is not part of the 'Safe Harbor' scheme, a separate agreement was reached.

Subject Access Request

A Subject Access Request (SAR) is the means by which an individual can find out what data about them are held by an organization. Note that some information requests which may initially appear to be simple enquiries, or which may appear to fall under the Freedom of Information Act or the Environmental Information Regulations, will in fact relate to personal data, and thus come within the remit of the DPA. If the data requested are personal data relating to the individual making the request, this should be treated as a SAR, but if, as is more likely, the request relates to other people's personal data, the provisions of the DPA regarding disclosure would apply. You must respond to a valid SAR within 40 calendar days, telling the individual what information about them you hold, and providing them with a copy of the information.

Validity

A valid SAR must be made in writing, although e-mail and fax count as equivalent. It would, however, be good practice to treat a verbal request as if it were valid, or at least to explain how to make a valid request. It is also reasonable to make the necessary adjustments to enable people with disabilities to make valid requests, where they might otherwise be disadvantaged in doing so, as well as providing the information in an appropriate format to allow them to use it (for example, Braille, large print, or a computer file which could be used in a text-to-speech application).

What you must provide

As a data controller, you must provide the information you hold about an individual, but not necessarily the documents containing that information. This should be the information you hold at the time you receive the request, although if at that time the information is under routine amendment, or is due for deletion, it is reasonable to provide the information you hold at the time at which you respond to the request. However, you may not amend or delete the information if this would not have been routine, and if your organization is subject to the FOIA, that would constitute an offence.

The information must be in an 'intelligible form', which means that an average person should be able to understand it. Codes, for example, should be explained, but handwriting would not have to be transcribed, nor would translation into another language be expected.

Time for compliance

In most cases, you have 40 calendar days to respond to a request, starting with the day following the day you receive the request. In some cases, you may have to ask for a clarification of the request, in which case the time does not begin until you receive the clarification, but you should not use this as a mechanism for extending the time you take to respond. The same provision applies with respect to fees.

Fees

An organization may charge a fee (currently £10 maximum) for providing information, although organizations holding health or education records may, under certain circumstances, charge up to £50. If a fee is payable, but has not been sent with the request, you should contact the requestor and inform them of the need for payment. The 40-day period for responding to the request does not begin until the payment is received.

Information about other people

Individuals may ask a third party, such as a friend or a solicitor, to make a SAR on their behalf, or it may be that someone with the authority to manage an adult's property or affairs makes such a request on their behalf. You need to be satisfied that the third party is entitled to such authority, although it is their responsibility to provide the evidence to substantiate their claim. The law allows the data controller to decide that the nature of the information is such that it is more appropriate that it be sent directly to the individual, who can then make the decision as to whether to share it with the third party.

Information about children

Personal data about a child belongs to them, and it is they who have the right of access to the data, although in the case of very young children, this right may be exercised by a parent or guardian. It is your responsibility to decide whether a child is mature enough to understand their rights, to understand what it means to make a request, and to interpret the resulting information. If so, the response should be to the child, rather than to anyone else. In cases where this is a difficult decision, the ICO recommends that you also consider:

- the child's level of maturity and their ability to make decisions like this
- the nature of the personal data
- any court orders relating to parental access or responsibility that may apply
- any duty of confidence owed to the child or young person
- any consequences of allowing those with parental responsibility access to the child's or young person's information (this is particularly important if there have been allegations of abuse or ill treatment)
- any detriment to the child or young person if individuals with parental responsibility cannot access this information
- any views the child or young person has on whether their parents should have access to information about them.

Information Commissioner's Office (2013h)

In Scotland, it is presumed in law that a child of the age of 12 or more is capable of making a SAR. Although this does not apply elsewhere in the UK, it would appear to set a reasonable guideline. The ICO also notes that capacity to make the request does not imply capacity to understand the implications of sharing the information, or to consent to doing so.

Obviously these are potentially very difficult decisions for the data controller to make, since so much is open to interpretation. It might be advisable to seek legal advice under these circumstances, or even to arrange an advisory visit from the ICO, in order to prepare for such an eventuality, if your organization routinely processes such information (Information Commissioner's Office, 2013i).

Information about others

It may be the case that in order to provide information about an individual, you would also have to provide personal information about other people. If the other parties give their permission, this is not a problem, but if their permission cannot be obtained, you must decide whether it is reasonable to provide the information without their consent. The Act states that you do not have to comply with the request unless the third party has given permission, or it is reasonable to comply without such permission. Again, this is a matter of weighing the rights of the person making the request against the rights of the third party, and you will need to take all the relevant circumstances into account.

Disproportionate effort

It may be that the effort involved in supplying a copy of the information held necessitates effort that is disproportionate to the benefits to the individual, in which case you do not have to supply a copy of the information in permanent form. This could be because of the volume of information, or because of the way in which it is held. For example, an individual's transactions with a shop of which they are a customer might be recoverable in detail for only the most recent accounting period, whereas recovering details of older transactions might take considerable effort. However, the waiver only applies to supplying the information in permanent form, not to the work involved in locating it. Because the right to information is so important, it would be very unusual for this to be a valid reason, and it would probably be possible to provide the information in some alternative manner.

Repeated or unreasonable requests

You do not have to answer again the same, or a very similar, request, unless a reasonable time has elapsed since the last time the request was made. This might depend on how sensitive the data is, why it is being processed or how frequently the data changes. However, there is no limit on the number of requests an individual can make to an organization.

Environmental Information Regulations (EIR)

The Environmental Information Regulations implement EC directive 2003/4/CE, itself a result of the Aarhus Convention, 1998, which was signed by the EU and the UK. They apply to 'public authorities' – local authorities, government departments, police, universities, the NHS and some bodies that carry out public works that affect the environment.

There is a presumption in favour of disclosure – you must disclose information unless there is a good reason not to.

You have obligations:

- actively to make the information available, by electronic means if possible, and
- to respond to requests, which could be from anyone.

There is a code of practice for fulfilling your obligations under EIR, the Code of Practice – Environmental Information Regulations 2004 (Information Commissioner's Office, 2005), and a code of practice (code 46) covering the responsibilities of public authorities under FOI and EIR (Ministry of Justice, 2012b) (see Figure 2.2). Whereas under

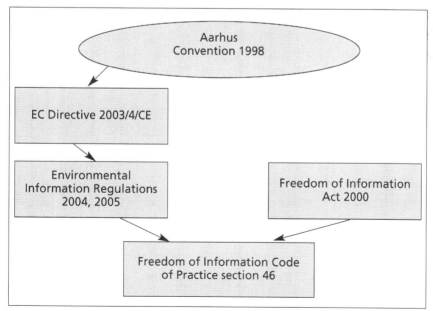

Figure 2.2 The code of practice derives from two sources of legislation

the FOIA you have a duty to maintain and publish a publication scheme, this does not apply under EIR, although it would appear to be a practice which would be consistent with the first obligation, and a way of demonstrating good practice.

According to the ICO, the minimum information you must routinely publish is listed in Article 7(2) of the European Directive 2003/4/EC. This includes policies, plans and procedures relating to the environment, reports on the state of the environment, environmental impact studies and data taken from monitoring activities and risk assessments that affect or are likely to affect the environment. This may cover public registers of environmental information you maintain under another piece of legislation, your organization's carbon emissions data, or details about external renovation and building work. You must also publish facts and analyses of facts that are relevant and important to major environmental policy proposals.

Copyright, database and intellectual property rights (IPR)

Disclosing information under EIR should not have any effect on these rights. You are not allowed to require people to sign a statement that they will not infringe copyright, although you may include a copyright notice with the information you do disclose, and you can make a claim in the courts regarding breaches of copyright. These rights considerations should not be a bar to disclosure, but there is an exemption to the disclosure requirement where disclosure could adversely affect IPR.

Property searches

Local Authorities (England) Charges for Property Searches Regulations (CPSR) is another potential area of overlap, since many property searches will be of an environmental nature, and the charging policies for each are different. The CPSR does not apply where the local authority (a) can charge for access to property records or (b) has to supply records free of charge under another enactment. If the information is environmental, EIR provides discretion for making a reasonable charge, and defines when the authority cannot charge.

What you must provide
Time for compliance

The information must be provided within 20 working days, beginning the day following the day that the organization receives the request, or the day following receipt of clarification of the original request, should this be required. It is good policy to refer to the time limit in the initial response to, or acknowledgement of, the request. If a request is particularly complex, an extension of up to an additional 20 days can be claimed, but in this case, the requestor should be told.

Fees

If a fee is to be charged, and advance payment is required, the 20-day period does not begin until the fee is received, which must be within 60 days of the original request.

Policy

In each chapter, we'll be discussing the contribution that it can make towards a comprehensive information governance and assurance policy for your organization. The main points arising from this chapter are the importance of good records management in responding to information requests, and the fact that much of the work involved can be carried out in advance, by publishing information actively.

The records retention schedule

It ought to be clear that compliance with the various regulations is desirable for a number of reasons. First, there are the ideals of openness and accountability which influenced the framing of the regulations in the first place. Second, providing the information is providing a public service, as is protecting it from misuse. Third, the ability to produce information on any relevant topic, at short notice and without compromising the normal operations of your organization, is a sign of a well organized and efficient approach to information management. Finally, avoidance of the quite considerable sanctions at the disposal of the ICO and its counterparts in other jurisdictions ought not to be the prime incentive towards compliance, but can certainly act as a spur.

It should be remembered that having a retention schedule is important for many reasons – the most obvious being that unneeded records aren't kept for longer than necessary, with the resultant waste of storage space, and perhaps increased difficulty in retrieving the records which *are* needed. Records retention requirements are not intended to hinder the carrying out of business, and it is not feasible to keep everything.

The retention schedule should list the different series of records, the person or department having 'ownership' of the records, the point at which they become 'inactive', and the method of their disposal – archiving or destruction. Each entry should also list the justification for this decision, which will usually be either a piece of legislation, advice from a body such as the Joint Information Systems Committee (Jisc) or the ICO, or organizational policy. When a record reaches the end of its useful life, the disposal routine should be triggered. In electronic records systems, this can often be done semi-automatically – but there should always be a human verification of the disposal. Retention times may vary widely – health records relating to those serving in HM Armed Forces are not to be destroyed, whereas the personal data of a survey subject should normally be disposed of on the termination of the survey.

In common with many public authorities, the ICO publishes its own records management policy (Ebitt, 2009), and it also discusses the benefits of a disposal schedule (Information Commissioner's Office, 2013j).

The publication scheme

Publication is required by the FOIA, and is not required, but is certainly advisable, under the EIR. You can save your requesters time and effort, and yourself time, effort and stress, by actively publishing, probably via a website, as much of the information as you can that would not be subject to an exemption. Obviously, this does not apply to personal information, where the emphasis is on accuracy and secure processing and disposal, but the same effort should be put into checking, organizing and making retrievable personal information as if it were to be published, because it is, but to a very restricted audience, typically of one.

The role of the information professional

There is a great deal of complexity discussed in this chapter, and there are many further ramifications to each piece of legislation which need to be considered. As an information professional, your role is quite likely to involve handling requests, or enquiries which might resolve to requests, in an efficient and effective manner. It would be a good idea to try to ensure that information requests, whether formal or not, are channelled through one authoritative point, which may well be your role. Other 'outward-facing' staff should be encouraged to channel requests in your direction, and it is quite easy to 'sell' this idea – they are helping the enquirer, but not taking on any additional work themselves. The data protection principles should certainly form part of staff induction or training in any public authority or other data controller.

Keeping abreast of the legislation is obviously important, and it is an area which is subject to fairly frequent updates.

Remember that the publication scheme is not an imposition, but a very useful tool – you do not want to spend all your working life 'firefighting'.

Finally, note that many of the enquiries you might receive can be dealt with informally, without ever reaching the status of a full-blown information request – this is good practice, and makes the whole process of access to information run much more smoothly for everyone involved.

∙∙

Discussion points

1 You work in the Planning Department of a local authority, and receive a request for any information you hold regarding planning applications by a particular individual for a property at a particular address. What would your response be?
2 What measures might you take to ensure the security of personal data held by your organization?
3 You work in a hospital, and are asked by the mother of a 14-year-old patient for details about his treatment. How should you respond?
4 As the curator of a military museum, you are asked for details of the service of a named individual who may have served in your

regiment at indeterminate dates. How should you respond?
5 The university in which you are the records manager receives an
enquiry about accidents related to harmful chemicals in the last
five years. What do you do?

••

Conclusion

In this chapter, we have dealt with the external drivers towards
information governance and assurance, and you should by now
understand that what might appear initially to be cumbersome laws
and regulations are in fact very necessary controls to dissuade
organizations from irresponsible information behaviour. In fact, this is
an instance of 'information assurance' – by complying with these rules
and regulations, we as an organization can feel assured that we are
doing the 'right thing' – acting responsibly towards individuals' data,
disclosing information about what we do on the public's behalf, if we
are a public body, in the public's interest, and being open about our
impact on the environment. We have also seen that bodies like Jisc and
the Information Commissioner's Office are an invaluable source of
plentiful and helpful advice. These organizations are there to help us
comply, rather than to persecute us for failure to do so.

All this means that, as individuals, we too can be assured in our
dealings with compliant organizations, that our best interests are being
looked after. There is no good reason for not observing these
regulations.

References

Best, D. (2002) *Effective Records Management: a management guide to the value of ISO
15489-1*, London, BSI.
The Data Protection (Processing of Sensitive Personal Data) Order 2000,
www.legislation.gov.uk/uksi/2000/417/schedule/made. [Accessed 08/06/13]
The Data Protection (Processing of Sensitive Personal Data) (Elected Representatives)
Order 2002, http://www.legislation.gov.uk/uksi/2002/2905/contents/made.
[Accessed 20/02/14]
Data Protection Act 1998, www.legislation.gov.uk/ukpga/1998/29/contents.
[Accessed 31/05/13]
Ebitt, S. (2009) *Records Management Policy*, Information Commissioner's Office,

www.ico.org.uk/˜/media/documents/library/Corporate/Notices/RECORDS_
MANAGEMENT_POLICY.ashx. [Accessed 19/06/13]

European Commission (2013) *Commission Decisions on the Adequacy of the Protection of
Personal Data in Third Countries*, http://ec.europa.eu/justice/data-protection/
document/international-transfers/adequacy/index_en.htm. [Accessed 09/06/13]

Export.gov (2012) *Main Safe Harbor homepage*, http://export.gov/safeharbor.
[Accessed 09/06/13]

Freedominfo.org (2013) *Rwanda Publishes New Law on Right to Information*,
www.freedominfo.org/2013/03/rwanda-publishes-new-law-on-right-to-information.
[Accessed 19/06/13]

Higgins, S. (2007) *ISO 15489*, Edinburgh, Digital Curation Centre, www.dcc.ac.uk/
resources/briefing-papers/standards-watch-papers/iso-15489. [Accessed 11/11/13]

Information Commissioner's Office (2005) *Code of Practice – Environmental Information
Regulations 2004*, http://ico.org.uk/for_organisations/guidance_index/˜/media/
documents/library/Environmental_info_reg/Detailed_specialist_guides/
ENVIRONMENTAL_INFORMATION_REGULATIONS_CODE_OF_PRACTICE.
ashx. [Accessed 17/06/13]

Information Commissioner's Office (2012a) *Public Authorities Under the Freedom of
Information Act*, http://ico.org.uk/˜/media/documents/library/ Freedom_of_
Information/Detailed_specialist_guides/public_authorities_under_ the_foia.pdf.
[Accessed 05/04/14]

Information Commissioner's Office (2012b) *Introduction to Principles 3, 4 and 5 of the
Data Protection Act*, http://ico.org.uk/for_organisations/data_protection/
the_guide/information_standards/introduction. [Accessed 08/06/13]

Information Commissioner's Office (2013a) *Enforcement*,
http://ico.org.uk/enforcement. [Accessed 30/05/13]

Information Commissioner's Office (2013b) *Model Publication Scheme*,
http://ico.org.uk/˜/media/documents/library/Freedom_of_Information/
Detailed_specialist_guides/model-publication-scheme.pdf. [Accessed 05/04/14]

Information Commissioner's Office (2013c) *When Can We Refuse a Request for
Information?*, http://ico.org.uk/for_organisations/freedom_of_information/
guide/refusing_a_request. [Accessed 30/05/13]

Information Commissioner's Office (2013d) *Key Definitions of the Data Protection Act*,
http://ico.org.uk/for_organisations/data_protection/the_guide/key_definitions.
[Accessed 30/03.14]

Information Commissioner's Office (2013e) *Register (Notify) under the Data Protection
Act*, http://ico.org.uk/for_organisations/data_protection/registration. [Accessed
08/06/13]

Information Commissioner's Office (2013f) *The Conditions for Processing*,
http://ico.org.uk/for_organisations/data_protection/the_guide/conditions_
for_processing. [Accessed 07/06/13]

Information Commissioner's Office (2013g) *Principle 6 of the Data Protection Act –
Guide to Data Protection*, http://ico.org.uk/for_organisations/data_protection/
the_guide/principle_6. [Accessed 09/06/13]

Information Commissioner's Office (2013h) *Access to Personal Data*, http://ico.org.uk/
for_organisations/data_protection/the_guide/principle_6/access_to_
personal_data. [Accessed 16/06/13]

Information Commissioner's Office (2013i) *Advisory Visits,* http://ico.org.uk/
what_we_cover/audits_advisory_visits_and_self_assessments/advisory_visits.
[Accessed 16/06/13]

Information Commissioner's Office (2013j) *Retention and Destruction of Requested
Information*, http://ico.org.uk/~/media/documents/library/Freedom_of_
Information/Practical_application/retention-and-destruction-of-requested-
information.pdf. [Accessed 05/04/14]

ISO/IEC (2001a) ISO 15489-1:2001 *Information and Documentation – Records Management
– Part 1: General*, Geneva, International Organization for Standardization.

ISO/IEC (2001b) ISO/TR 15489-2:2001 *Information and Documentation – Records
Management – Part 2: Guidelines*, Geneva, International Organization for
Standardization.

Jones, P. (2003) *Effective Records Management: performance management for BS ISO
15489-1*, London, BSI.

Kuner, C. (2010) Data Protection Law and International Jurisdiction on the Internet
(Part 1), *International Journal of Law and Information Technology*, 18 (2), 176–93,
http://ijlit.oxfordjournals.org/content/18/2/176.full.pdf+html. [Accessed
19/06/13]

McLeod, J. (2002) *Effective Records Management: practical implementation of ISO 15489-1*,
London, BSI.

Ministry of Justice (2012a) *Neither Confirm Nor Deny*, www.justice.gov.uk/information-
access-rights/foi-guidance-for-practitioners/exemptions-guidance/foi-exemptions-
ncnd. [Accessed 17/06/13]

Ministry of Justice (2012b) *Freedom of Information Code of Practice*, www.justice.gov.uk/
information-access-rights/foi-guidance-for-practitioners/code-of-practice.
[Accessed 17/06/13]

Penn, I. A., Pennix, G. B. and Coulson, J. (1994) *Records Management Handbook*,
Cambridge, Cambridge University Press.

US National Archives and Records Administration (2005) *NARA Guidance on Managing and Maintaining Web Records*, www.archives.gov/records-mgmt/policy/managing-web-records.html. [Accessed 12/11/13]

CHAPTER 3

Data quality management

On two occasions I have been asked [by members of Parliament!], 'Pray, Mr Babbage, if you put into the machine wrong figures, will the right answers come out?' I am not able rightly to apprehend the kind of confusion of ideas that could provoke such a question.

Charles Babbage (Babbage, 1864, 67)

Introduction

We looked in the last chapter at the importance of making sure that the data that some organizations hold and supply on various topics are accurate, up to date, not excessive and secure in both their storage and disposal. It is important, though, to remember that, while not all organizations are in the public sector, and not all organizations are data controllers in the eyes of the law, all organizations have a reliance on the quality of their data that extends beyond mere compliance. This chapter deals with the growing importance of data quality in the operation of organizations, and at how data consistency, validity and quality can best be maintained. Although the term 'databases' is frequently used in this chapter, it is important to remember that our concern is not only with relational databases and database management systems, such as Oracle, MySQL or Microsoft Access. Many of the information systems we depend on, such as spreadsheets, or even text documents, are 'flat file' databases – holding multiple instances of the same record type.

Many systems which are represented as performing quite individual and specialized functions, for example customer relationship management (CRM), content management systems (CMS), or enterprise resource planning (ERP) systems are, in fact, databases with a sophisticated user interface. Another example is integrated library management systems (ILMS). An actual database management system makes it easier to handle and to perform operations on large amounts of data, but any information professional will rely on something which is, effectively, a database, and the points made in this chapter apply to all of these.

The impact of large databases and the application of data quality tools are discussed, and the importance of a data quality policy is stressed. This is primarily an internal issue for the organization – the next chapter deals with external threats.

There is an international standard, ISO8000 – Data Quality, but this is primarily concerned with standards to be expected from data exchanged between organizations. In this chapter, we are mainly dealing with the internal effects of data quality, so we will not discuss the standard further, but it is worth noting that it might be of relevance to the operations of some types of organization, who might wish to be certified as suppliers of quality data, for example, and it could easily be built into the framework discussed in Chapter 6.

What is data quality?

The notion of data having 'quality' is not, perhaps, one with which most people are familiar, so it may be helpful to begin with some examples of what happens when data quality is insufficient. One with which most of us will be familiar is when our name is misspelled on a letter. I receive letters for: 'Allan', 'Allen', 'Alun'; 'Maclennan', 'McLennan', 'MacLelland', 'McKellern', 'McClennen' and other variations, and mine is not a particularly complex name. Apart from causing momentary annoyance, that seems a trivial mistake – someone has misheard, misremembered, or simply cannot spell the name, and the addition of a postcode, or the local knowledge of a postal worker, gets the letter delivered. If the letter is 'junk mail', I may even be relieved, because I have a sense that the sender does not really have me on file – this is not my 'real identity'. However, if the communication is about something important, such as a bank account, or a utilities bill, or an electoral register, then it becomes of greater concern. This letter may have arrived, by luck, but were there others which did not? Can I even correct the mistake, since this isn't 'really me'?

When computers are introduced to the scenario, other problems may emerge. My surname is 'MacLennan', and in a conventionally ordered printed list, such as might be found in a telephone directory, the variant form 'McLennan' would be inter-filed:

MacLennan, A.
McLennan, B.
MacLennan, C.

However, if the ordering is left to a computer, names of each type of spelling will be grouped together:

MacLennan, A.
MacLennan, C.
MacLennan, W.
. . .
MacNiven, L.
. . .
MacPherson, D.
. . .
McLean, M.
. . .
McLennan, B.
McLennan, F.

Obviously, this may cause confusion for the searcher who is used to one style, when faced with the other. Another form of personal name occurring frequently in the names of streets, towns and cities is 'Saint', or 'St.', or 'St' (without the dot signifying abbreviation).

Of course, 'St.' and 'St' are also used as abbreviations for 'Street', and we have 'Dr' for 'Drive' (and 'Doctor'), 'Ct' for 'Court' (and perhaps 'Count') and so on. Different people will use different representations, as may the same person at different times, depending on what they are transcribing.

For example, if you were conducting a survey by interviewing passers-by in a town centre, you might be more likely to use the most abbreviated form you could think of at the time. However, if someone is writing an address into a form, or typing it into a form on a web page, they may have a favourite style that they use, or they may be constrained by the space available, or they may be copying in what someone else has written. All these and other circumstances can lead to variation in the data, which in turn can lead to mismatching and to duplicate records.

Am I, 'Alan MacLennan', the same person as an 'Alan McLennan' recorded at the same address? That seems like an obvious case of a duplicate record – two records referring to the same entity – me. But what if the address is that of a large organization, or a student hall of residence, or nurses' home? Then the probability that there is more than one individual becomes greater.

So far, we have only considered data elements concerning names and addresses, and only some of the more obvious problems with these. More will emerge later, when we look at how they can be remedied, but first it will be helpful to try to impose some structure on the problem.

Dimensions of data quality

When discussing data quality, many authors refer to 'dimensions' – axes or scales of measurement of different aspects of quality, which may, but do not necessarily, bear some relation to each other.

Some characteristics of data quality are accuracy, completeness, consistency and timeliness. These provide some common ground for discussion and theorizing, although Chisholm (2012) and Myers (2013) amongst others, note that there are inconsistencies in the definitions and usage of these 'dimensions' by different authors.

Accuracy

Accuracy, or syntactic accuracy, to be more precise, has to do with the correspondence of data values to some value considered to be 'correct' – often a 'real-world' value. Semantic accuracy, on the other hand, is what we have when the data value is of the right type, or comes from the correct domain, rather than necessarily having the correct value.

To return to my name travails, recording my surname as 'McLennan', perhaps in an entry for this book in a bibliographic database, would be a syntactic inaccuracy – there is an 'edit distance' of 1 between that value and the 'real-world' value of 'MacLennan', which can be resolved by the insertion of the letter 'a'. If the value stored was 'Reid', then that would be a semantic inaccuracy – the data type is correct, the value is a possible value, but it does not correspond to the 'real world' situation.

What are the reasons for inaccuracy, and how can we mitigate against it? Often, the cause will be simple human error – someone will complete a form with misspelled or incorrect details, because their memory lets them down, or they're in a hurry, and can't be bothered to check the facts, or they enter data in the wrong place, whether by hand or on a web page. How many employees are there in your organization? What is your organization's annual budget for software? You may, like me, tick the first checkbox that seems reasonable, without bothering to check the facts, because all you want to do is read a 'free' report, but somewhere, someone is dealing with inaccurate data, because of our laziness. Or maybe the correct option isn't available. I often find, when completing the type of form required to gain access to 'free' 'white papers' (usually thinly disguised advertising material), that although 'Education' is quite often an option for the type of business that my organization is involved in, it is much less often the case that 'Lecturer' or any equivalent job title is offered as an option. Since the form validation rules require all fields to be completed, I try to find something 'close', but, to be honest, I do not try very hard. The organization is getting what it wants – more or less – which is my e-mail address and some demographic data of variable quality, and I get to read their advertising, perhaps learning something of value in the process.

However, I am not an employee of the organization publishing the 'white paper', and, even in our age of a dramatic increase in 'crowd-sourcing', the organization may not have a right to expect the same standards of accuracy as they would from an employee. Employees, though, are just as susceptible to poor memory, carelessness or human error. The advantage that we have with data input by an employee is that it tends to be more controlled than that input by an 'outsider'. Part of the reason that I have difficulty finding an appropriate job description on some web forms is that I am an atypical customer. These firms want to sell software, or hardware, or other services, and tailor their web forms towards potential customers, who are influential in making budget decisions. My interest in the material is simply that I want to keep up to date, or so that I can use it in teaching – we are somewhat at cross purposes. An employee, however, is more likely to be dealing with part of a known data set – the details of a supplier or a customer, an order from a defined range of products, a particular set of payment options. For many years, online public access library catalogues (OPACs) have been making use of metadata to simplify the input of catalogue records. For example, when the cataloguer enters an author's name, or a title, or the name of a publisher, close matches already on the system can be displayed, with a prompt to either choose an existing name, or to confirm that the name is a new one. This has two benefits – it requires some thought, so that the decision is more likely to be a considered one, and it enables the use of an 'authority file' – a list of agreed definitive forms of names, titles, etc. Some authority files will hold only metadata local to the system, but there are international name authority files, which considerably increase the accuracy of author identification.

That term, 'metadata', is central to the accuracy issue. It is usually defined as 'data about data', and organizing metadata is, in a sense, what cataloguing is concerned with. Metadata, though, is really how we keep any kind of control over the data we deal with. If a set of data comprising a document can be assigned the correct metadata, we 'have a handle on it' – we have controlled the routes by which it may be edited, stored, retrieved, archived or deleted. So, as simple a process as providing a selection of potentially useful metadata from which to choose at a data input stage can reduce inaccuracy.

Of course, these measures have to be accompanied by staff training, and the encouragement of a culture that recognizes the importance of metadata, something which cataloguers have emphasized for many years.

Completeness

Completeness can be thought of as defining the degree to which the data describe the entity they are 'about'. At the 'collection' level, do we have a record for every item in the collection? At the item level, are the data for each item complete? If a datum is missing from a record, there may be several reasons, not all of which affect the completeness of the record. For example, a web form may have a space in which a person's mobile phone number can be entered. If the person has no mobile phone, and the space is left blank (in database terms, this is a 'null', having no value), the record is not incomplete. However, if the person does have a mobile phone number, but we do not know what it is, we may wish to consider that record incomplete. Or we may not know whether the person has a number or not. It is then our decision whether to treat the record as incomplete. However, it would not be a good idea to have completion of this field as part of a validity check on completing a web form, unless perhaps the form was intended for customers of a telephone service provider.

Consistency

The consistency dimension concerns the need for data to be consistent with each other – that is, they must agree, and when considered together, provide a picture which is not at odds with the world as represented by the data. We most often see this expressed as constraints on the data entered into tables in a relational database – 'if hasDrivingLicence is 'Yes', age must be >= 16', or 'if vehicleType = 'Motorcycle', numWheels = 2'. These are termed 'inter-relational constraints', because they concern the values in one 'relation' – the formal name for a table, from which the term 'relational database' is derived. Relations in a well designed database are 'about' one thing, one entity in the universe with which the database is concerned. So, having an age and (perhaps) a driving licence are attributes of a person, being a motorcycle and having a number of wheels are attributes of a vehicle. We can also have inter-relational constraints. Suppose that we have a relation (or table) representing students, which has an attribute (or field) in each record (or tuple) holding the code of the course on which the student is enrolled. An inter-relational constraint might specify that the course code in each student record be a valid code from the course table. Some breaches of consistency may be amenable to automatic correction, and any breaches can at least be identified as requiring checking.

Real-world examples of consistency issues

Another kind of consistency issue became dramatically apparent in 1999, when the US National Aeronautics and Space Administration (NASA) lost an unmanned craft orbiting Mars. The craft was instructed to enter the Martian atmosphere, but because the attitude-control system used imperial units (feet and pounds) whilst the navigation software used metric units (metres and kilos), it was 100 kilometres too close to the surface, and crashed. The craft cost $125 million. NASA has a long-standing problem relating to its continued use of imperial measurements, and in 2006 its DART spacecraft collided with a military satellite with which it was meant to dock, because a correction intended to make its GPS software read in metres rather than in feet (a problem discovered before launch) interfered with another parameter in the software and led to the collision. It even appears that NASA's plans for commercial exploitation of the successor to the Space Shuttle may have been set back because of their institutional commitment to 'legacy' imperial measurements. The cost of conversion would apparently be more than they could afford, despite a 2004 directive to move towards 'International System' (SI) units (Marks, 2009).

Another example was related by a student who worked for an oil company which had bought from another company the rights to an oil field and the data resulting from its exploration. Because the data were in a proprietary format belonging to an obsolete software package, and had been collected by a company which no longer existed, there were considerable problems associated with their use. One problem led to a well being drilled in the wrong place – a small distance, but still costing many millions of dollars. Because of perceived loss of reputation and competitive business intelligence, organizations may well decide not to publicize incidents of this kind. This leads one to wonder what the costs of data quality problems really amount to.

Timeliness

Timeliness encompasses at least three 'time-related' ideas – timeliness, currency and volatility. Batini and Scannapieca (2006, 40) compare statements about these made in seven influential works in the field, and find that 'There is not even agreement on the semantics of a specific dimension: indeed, for timeliness, different meanings are provided by different authors'. So, without any attempt to be authoritative, but more to try to communicate the idea behind each term, 'timeliness' has something to do with how well up to date the data is; how quickly it reflects changes in the real-world situation. It will, as will all the terms, vary according to the scenario – the scales will be much different for stock market prices, prices of goods in a shop, and property prices in the housing market. This is similar to the definition given by Wand and Wang (1996), but is also very similar to the definition of 'currency' given by Redman (1997). For Jarke et al. (1999) and Bovee, Srivastava and Mak (2001), currency is simply concerned with when the data was entered. Volatility for Jarke is the period for which information is valid, whilst Bovee considers it to be the frequency with which data changes. Or we could ask, are these data the latest available? Are they 'in time' for whatever they're needed for?

Reasonability

Sebastian-Coleman (2013, 49) adds a further means of gauging data quality – the 'reasonability check', which 'provides a means of drawing a conclusion about data based on knowledge of data content rather than on a strictly numeric measurement'. It amounts to asking whether the data make sense, based on what you know about them. Sebastian-Coleman gives an example of a collection of employee data which shows one employee to be aged 130, according to a datum about his birthdate. This is clearly unreasonable, whereas employee ages less than 18 are sufficiently unusual to merit further investigation.

A different perspective

Wang, Strong and Guarascio (1994) found that information systems professionals regarded quality as being principally concerned with accuracy. They conducted a study which attempted to establish factors in data quality which were important to data consumers. By a progressive sorting and grouping of terms derived from the data consumers and related to data quality, they developed a hierarchical framework, which reduces the many labels used by consumers to four 'facets', allowing us to tackle a manageable number of aspects (Table 3.1).

Table 3.1 Data quality (after Wang, Strong and Guarascio, 1994)			
Intrinsic data quality	Contextual data quality	Representation data quality	Accessibility data quality

Believability
Accuracy
Objectivity
Reputation
	Value-added
	Relevancy
	Timeliness
	Completeness
	Appropriate
	    amount of data
		Interpretability
		Ease of
		    understanding
		Representational
		    consistency
		Concise
		    representation
			Accessibility
			Access security

Here we can see the conventional set of dimensions – accuracy, completeness, consistency, timeliness – which are identified by the majority of authors, and one can see that dimensions which are identified less frequently, like objectivity, relevancy or representational quality, have been found 'homes' in appropriate groupings of the hierarchy. This kind of arrangement is of value in that it enables us to grasp better the classes of concepts under discussion. Wang, Strong and Guarascio began with 179 data quality attributes suggested by the data consumers, which were rated by importance, reduced to remove synonyms and sorted into groups, in further iterations of the study.

Example

At this point, it may be helpful to consider an example (Figure 3.1) used by Batini and Scannapieca (2006, 5). If we consider a simple flat-file database containing records for publications, we can illustrate some issues affecting the various 'dimensions'.

The title of film 3 is syntactically inaccurate, because it does not correspond to the name of a film in the 'real world'. There is an 'edit distance' of 1 between this and the 'real' title, 'Roman Holiday', which

ID	Title	Director	Year	#Remakes	Year last remade
1	Casablanca	Weir	1942	3	1940
2	Dead Poets Society	Curtiz	1982	0	NULL
3	Rman Holiday	Wyler	1953	0	NULL
4	Sabrina	NULL	1964	0	1985

Figure 3.1 (from Batini and Scannapieca 2006, 5)
© Reproduced with kind permission of Springer Science+Business Media.

corresponds to the single edit of replacing the 'o' as the second letter. The directors of films 1 and 2 have been transposed, so, although each is syntactically accurate – there are such directors, these are valid directors' names – they do not correspond to the 'real world', and so are semantically inaccurate.

The director of film 4 is missing, which is a completeness problem, and the number of remakes for film 4 demonstrates a currency problem because (according to Batini and Scannapieca) a remake has been proposed. Also with respect to film 4, there is an inconsistency between the number of remakes and the year last remade, which should be NULL. There is another inconsistency in the record for film 1 – the year last remade should not be earlier than the year of release.

Having looked at very small-scale examples of some of the problems which can arise with data, the next step is to consider what can be done to remediate them.

Batini et al. (2009) distinguish between data-driven and process-driven initiatives towards data quality improvement. The first type of initiative directly modifies the values of data, the second type modifies the processes by which data are acquired and processed. Batini et al. define dimensions as including accuracy, completeness, consistency and timeliness, these 'constituting the focus of the majority of authors' (16:6). So, if we conduct a survey of data quality, and identify shortfalls, an obvious first step is correction. However, this is just treating the symptom, and it would be preferable to stop the shortfalls occurring, which will probably entail changes to the ways that data are collected and/or processed.

Data quality tools

In 2012, Gartner conducted a survey of data quality tools, and found that 'demand . . . remains strong, driven by more deployments that support information governance programs, master data management initiatives and application modernization efforts' (Gartner, 2012). We shall be moving on to look at some process-driven initiatives later, but first we shall consider the tools.

'Data quality assurance is a discipline focused on assuring that data is fit for use in business processes, ranging from core operations, to analytics and decision-making, to engagement and interaction with external entities' (Gartner, 2012).

Gartner regards 'the core functional requirements of the discipline' as:

- profiling
- parsing and standardization
- generalized 'cleansing'
- matching
- monitoring
- enrichment.

In this chapter, the order of the last two will be reversed, since monitoring is part of maintenance, an ongoing process which is necessary to ensure that progress is carried on into the future, and that feedback is gathered and acted upon.

Profiling

Profiling is concerned with deriving metadata to determine to what extent the data needs modification – what problems are there? Sebastian-Coleman (2013) has constructed a data quality assessment framework (DQAF) which comprises 48 measurement types related to dimensions of quality, each with a logical model, support processes required to use the measurement results, the business concerns the measurement addresses, a methodology, programming required to take the measurements and process results. There are six facets: definition, business concerns, measurement methodology, engineering and programming support, processes and skills, and measurement logical data model (Sebastian-Coleman, 2013, 220). The framework emphasizes prioritizing measurement types and carrying out an ongoing process of measurement. Obviously, this is a very rigorous approach, and in many organizations, a great deal of headway can be made by a less formal approach – simply talking to the various data 'owners' about how they work and what their problems are, and to the IT department about recurrent problems, especially those which cross departmental boundaries, ought to be enough to identify the problems which most concern people, and could lead to 'quick wins'.

Parsing and standardization

Parsing breaks down text fields into their components, just like parsing a sentence in a language class, when it is broken down into nouns, verbs, clauses, etc. An example involving data might be identification of the country code and area code components of a telephone number. (A telephone number can be treated as a text field, because numeric operations, such as addition and multiplication, are not performed upon it.) Standardizing reformats those components into a form compliant with standards – perhaps the postal address standards required by the US Postal Service. The standards might be industry standards, such as part numbers for engine components, or defined locally by a particular organization. These types of standardization might be most needed when merging departments from two or more existing organizations, as could be the case following a merger or acquisition.

Generalized 'cleansing'

Generalized 'cleansing' means changing data values so that they fall within acceptable domains, or satisfy integrity constraints, so that the data is of sufficient quality for the organization to work with. For example, delivery dates should not be earlier than order dates, month names or numbers must fall within the conventional range of 12, and so on. Some operations might be considered as being more strictly concerned with accuracy or consistency, but the label can include operations such as ensuring that the title element in a name falls within an acceptable range (e.g. 'Mr', 'Mrs', 'Ms', 'Dr').

The other step that can be taken is data validation – are dates valid dates, both in their format (only valid day numbers for each month, no 30th February, for instance) and in their relation to each other (end date/time must be later than start date/time)? For example, you might apply rules converting MM/DD/YYYY style dates in some of your input data to DD/MM/YYYY, or vice versa (IBM, 2009). This can be automated, as can checks for valid e-mail addresses, based on the pattern of where the @ sign is, and where the delimiting dots are. Checks for correct and existing e-mail addresses can be done fairly easily by the automated e-mailing of a registration link or password. Checks for the presence of required values can be automated by adding JavaScript to web pages, or by identifying fields as 'required' in web authoring packages.

Matching

Matching is a process which begins with identifying records which are related, perhaps because they refer to the same individual, and may progress to link or merge such records.

A possible solution for what we might call the 'variant data problem' is 'canonicalization', by which variant forms are converted to a single, authoritative form, the name coming from the 'canon' of Biblical texts held by Christian churches to be Holy Scripture. As we have seen, this will not work for names, because there are genuine, equally valid spellings. However, we could convert all instances of 'St' or 'St.' to 'Street', 'Cr' to 'Crescent', 'Rd' to 'Road' and so on, on the basis that the spelled-out form is least ambiguous. We need not do this by hand – a simple script in a programming language such as Perl could do this with great speed. What could possibly go wrong?

One of our university premises was on 'St Andrew St'. The first 'St' is an abbreviation for 'Saint', the second for 'Street'. It is very often transcribed as 'St Andrew's St', which is another problem, but for the moment, let us just stay with the 'St's. If both of those are expanded to

'Street', we have 'Street Andrew Street', which is incorrect. Expanding both to 'Saint' will not work, either. A very similar problem will arise with 'Dr Ross Dr.' – one 'Doctor', one 'Drive'.

The program needs a bit more sophistication, and Perl, as well as other languages using 'regular expressions', can deal easily with converting to 'Street' only those instances of 'St' (and 'St.') which come at the end of an address line, and converting others to 'Saint'. Of course, we will then encounter addresses such as 'Baker St Mews', and these may have to be dealt with by comparison with a street directory, where one is available. The point is that it is not as trivial an exercise as it may at first appear, and so far, we have only considered names and addresses for existing people and places.

Soares (2011), in a chapter dealing with the insurance industry, makes some interesting points about preferred sources of information when merging incomplete or contradictory records for different types of insurance policy under the identity of the common policyholder. In this context, the 'definitive' source for date of birth data would be the life policy, because the date of birth of the insured is central to the policy, the premiums being based on the date of birth. Address and telephone number, however, are more reliably taken from property insurance, since they 'belong' to the property insured.

Enrichment

Enrichment involves the improvement of records held by the organization, by adding in data from other sources. For example, postcode data captured from the purchasers of a particular service might be enriched by associating them with demographic data about the social status of residents of the area, such as that obtained from the widely used (in the UK) National Readership Survey (NRS) scale, which codes the upper and middle classes as 'ABC1'. Credit rating information can be purchased and used to enrich records of customers or prospects.

Another form of data enhancement would be to take customers' postcodes or zip codes, and add to that information from another source, such as census records. From the census records for 2011, for

Scotland, we can find the percentage of people living alone, the percentage in age groups 0–15, 15–64 and over 65. We can also find the population density for each area, and the number of households. The US Census Bureau collects and publishes data, by area code, on race – 'American Indian or Alaska Native,' 'Asian,' 'Black or African American,' 'Native Hawaiian or Other Pacific Islander,' and 'White' – and ethnicity – 'Hispanic or Latino' and 'Not Hispanic or Latino.' Race and Hispanic origin are treated as two separate concepts in the Federal system (United States Census Bureau, 2013) and it is possible that this information might be of use in targeting advertising of particular products or services.

Web logs are a potential source for enrichment. These are files maintained by the web server program (such as Apache) which record details of all requests coming into the server. Every time someone types in a URL, or clicks on a link, for our website, quite a lot of information is recorded. We can find where users are, geographically, what browser they use, when they access the site, where, if anywhere, they have reached the site from (did they arrive via a link from another site?), what pages they look at, how long they spend on the site – all potentially valuable information. If the site is used for sales, what did they buy? What else did they buy with it, and what have they bought previously?

This kind of user profiling is moving towards the territory often known as 'data mining', a specialized field in itself, but one which is, again, reliant on high-quality data. It is an example of the pervasive influence of the use of large databases, by which we are all affected. Data gathered from your browsing history on the web, from your use of 'loyalty cards', credit and debit cards, your responses to e-mails, your similarities to 'customers who viewed this' in online stores – all these, and many more sources are used to enrich records about you, and to target you with more tailored advertising, amongst other, and perhaps more sinister, purposes. However, as we have seen, publicly accessible large databases can also be used by the smaller operator – a quick web search can often turn up an elusive telephone number, e-mail, or the photograph that enables you to identify someone.

A library example

An example of enrichment from a library context concerns the enrichment of bibliographic records. One of the reports offered by some integrated library systems is a 'missed keywords' report, which lists search terms entered by users, but which have not resulted in a 'hit' – no corresponding records have been found. In addition to broadening the vocabulary of library staff, this report can be useful in enriching the catalogue. It can show where words are commonly misspelled, and might be automatically corrected, or at least queried, in the polite Google manner: 'Did you mean *x*?' Where the terms are not obvious misspellings, their use indicates that users are searching for material which is not indexed under those terms. In that case, either there is no material on that topic, which may justify examination of the collection and the acquisitions policy, or the material is there, but is not indexed using those terms, which may justify examination and perhaps extension of the indexing practices.

Monitoring

Monitoring, as the name suggests, is an ongoing process of ensuring that data continue to meet acceptable standards. The US Postal Service and the UK Royal Mail both maintain National Change of Address (NCOA) registers, storing the names and old and new addresses of customers who have asked that their mail be redirected. In the USA, the data are sold to organizations, who can obtain a preferential mailing rate for having checked the addresses they use against the database. In the UK, the database is not sold directly, but organizations' address data may be corrected by licensed agencies, who charge for the service. Versions of the NCOA system are also used in other countries, including Austria, Belgium, Canada, France, Germany, Australia and New Zealand. We should not assume, having obtained a complete and satisfactory data set regarding an entity, that it is now a fixed asset. Addresses may change, as may part numbers and codes, models in production, items in print, staff who are employed – just about any data set you can think of is subject to change, and should therefore be subject to review. An example which is forgotten more often than it ought to be is outdated links on web pages. They may not be a conventional data set, and they are probably not stored in a database anywhere, but broken links on a web page reflect badly on the page's owner. Hyperlinks are quite easy to check, and free automated link checking programs and services are available.

Data scrubbing

Maintenance of data quality can be helped by periodic 'scrubbing' of data – systematically applying updates (have your supplier's contact details changed? Have they been updated on all your systems?), standardization (are all dates, telephone numbers, physical data stored in the same format, units, fields in a record?), and deduplication (are there similar, but not identical, records naming an individual or an organization in different styles?). Automated tools can be used to save time in repetitive tasks such as checking for incomplete data and, for example, inserting missing postcodes or zip codes, or identifying and removing instances of duplicate records.

Loshin (2012) provides an extensive discussion of the principles behind manipulating address data, and details some of the uses to which the enhanced data may be put. He uses address data because they are both an example of data which commonly need to be 'cleaned up' and a data set with which we are all familiar, but his points are applicable to other data sets, too. Dempsey gives us an instance of name and identity data, as the subject of projects involving OCLC, amongst others:

> The source of information about names in the above initiatives is the creator themselves, or expert metadata creators. However, we also expect to complement this work by programmatically identifying names. We are exploring automatic recognition, extraction, and disambiguation of named entities (e.g., the names of people, places, and organizations) from digital texts. This work will be increasingly important, as manual description methods will not scale.
>
> Dempsey (2013)

Deduplication reduces redundancy, which is good, according to relational database design principles, which hold that a piece of datum should only be stored in one place, and that all other uses of that datum should be resolved by reference to that one instance. This reduces Create, Retrieve, Update and Delete (CRUD) errors. It can also reduce storage requirements quite significantly. Suppose that some department in your organization decides to send every member of staff their own copy of the new health and safety manual in a portable document format (PDF) file, as an e-mail attachment. Of course, we know from the previous chapter that the document would be better placed on a website, and links sent by e-mail, so that the document can be updated in a single place, and is available to any enquirers who might otherwise send a request under the Freedom of Information Act, but these ideas can take some time to permeate all departments. Now, all our employees have identical copies of a large document in their personal e-mail mailbox, and the document is 'read-only', in the sense that no one will be editing it. Therefore, a deduplicating program could replace each of these documents with a link to a single instance of the document, with considerable saving of space.

Data integration

Another way of approaching this problem is by considering it as 'data integration'. Batini and Scannapieca (2006) give the example of a bank, which may have many different registers of its customers, compiled and updated by different procedures. This could make provision of an accurate list of a customer's holdings problematic. Mergers and acquisitions may also result in data from different sources, recorded in different ways and with differing levels of completeness and reliability, having to be brought together and rationalized. So far, we've used examples drawn from customer data, but the merger and acquisition scenario might relate equally well to manufacturing data and processes, medical records, or core sample data from drilling operations.

In addition to these core requirements, which, as you can see, cover the range of operations we might want to undertake to improve data quality, some packages offer more specialized functionality, dealing, perhaps, with internationalization, specialization for particular subject areas or connectivity with different data structures.

The top-performing packages in the survey are perhaps not quite 'household names', but they are certainly familiar in the world of business information: (in no particular order) SAS/Dataflux, Informatica, IBM, Trillium and SAP.

Case study – PDSA

In the UK, the People's Dispensary for Sick Animals (PDSA) is a charity which funds veterinary care for the animals of owners who cannot themselves afford the costs. They rely entirely on public donations, and hence are very reliant on mailings.

This happens on a very large scale:

> During 2006, the IT team processed more than 46 million records and PDSA mailed over 15 million items. Mailings range from individual letters and direct mail pieces tailored to the supporters' preferences, to the magazine 'Companions', which is sent out on a quarterly basis to regular givers.
> Experian QAS (2013)

Managing large quantities of contact data can lead to problems of inaccuracy – for example, an address and postcode might be mis-matched – and duplication – for example, more than one address might be held for a donor, but only one is their preferred delivery address, a preference which the PDSA feels it has a duty to respect.

The first problem is handled by periodically running the organization's Oracle database of addresses against Experian QAS's enhanced version of the Royal Mail's Postcode Address File (PAF).

> Postcode information is made available to individual members of the public free of charge through Royal Mail's Postcode Finder service. The Postcode Address File is also made available to all businesses and organizations through a flexible licensing mechanism that helps towards paying for the considerable and on-going investment in the maintenance and provision of the dataset.
> Royal Mail Group (2013)

The Royal Mail announced in 2013 its intention to make the PAF freely available to independent small charities (those of less than £10m per annum income, and who are not associated or affiliated with an existing solutions provider) and to micro-businesses (fewer than ten employees, and less than £2m annual turnover), so that they can develop 'PAF-based products and take them to market' (Royal Mail Group, 2013). In addition to increasing the number of free look-ups of the PAF available to the public from 15 to 50 per day and other licensing concessions, this move highlights the Royal Mail's interest in encouraging the use of correct postcodes, whilst still recouping money from commercial licensing. Indeed, another incentive for the PDSA to run this check on their data is that they can get discounted postage rates on deliveries to addresses which have been so checked. They claim to save 'a million pounds a year on mailing alone' (Experian QAS, 2013).

The organization can use the same process for checking address data sets they may be considering purchasing, in order to negotiate a more favourable price, based on an assessment of inaccuracies and duplications. The data is then subject to 'further in-house data enhancements and profiling' so that preferred addresses can be used, and owners can even be selected according to the type of pet they own (Experian QAS, 2013). We have already seen examples of other enhancements which might be made.

When the savings in postage and the potential gains in effectiveness are taken into account, the PDSA would appear to be deriving considerable benefits from focusing on this single, rather prosaic, aspect of their data.

Products versus processes

It could be argued that measures like these constitute 'closing the stable door after the horse has bolted', and that, rather than simply dealing with existing unsatisfactory data (which will still remain a first step) we should look to implement processes which provide high-quality data in the first place. Opposition to this approach is likely to arise on two fronts. First, it will almost certainly be time-consuming and expensive to implement new processes, rather than 'work-arounds' which may have the perceived advantage of familiarity. In a sense, it's 'easier' to write a program to convert between date formats in existing data than to redesign and integrate the various input methods which have led to the discrepancy. Secondly, the changes may turn out to be larger and more fundamental than they at first appear, and the organization may find itself engaged in business process re-engineering (BPR) – not an activity to be undertaken lightly.

Case study – Nestlé

A case study of BPR at Nestlé SA reveals some interesting points regarding both data quality and BPR. Nestlé, a large food and pharmaceuticals organization, had reached a point in 1999 where it had revenues of US$46.6 billion, 230,000 employees in 500 plants in 80 countries, and worldwide recognition of its brands of milk, coffee and confectionery products. It also sells thousands of other items, most of which are adapted to suit local markets and cultures. These range from green tea-flavoured KitKat for the Japanese market (Madden, 2010), to a blend of coffee with lots of milk and sugar for the Chinese market (Wang Chao, 2012). This localization has resulted in very specific and very successful marketing, but the decentralized approach led to it having 80 different information technology (IT) units, running 15 mainframe computers, nearly 900 IBM AS/400 midrange computers and 200 UNIX systems. There was no corporate computing centre.

Nestlé's management found that the local variations created inefficiencies and extra costs that could have been preventing the company from competing effectively in electronic commerce. Because business processes were not standardized across the company, it was unable to take advantage of its considerable worldwide buying power to get better deals for its raw materials, and, even though each factory used the same global suppliers, each factory negotiated its own deals and prices separately.

When Nestlé decided to embark on a business process re-engineering project in the late 1990s, a study of the organization's strengths and weaknesses discovered that, for example, different plants in the company were paying the same vendor 29 different prices for the same ingredient, vanilla. This had come about because each plant negotiated individually with the vendor, and obtained the best deal it could at the time. Also, divisions and factories had named the same products differently, so that comparisons could not be made across the company. There were nine different general ledgers, 28 points of customer entry and multiple purchasing systems. The company decided to use SAP software, and the project, which initially failed for reasons generally attributed to poor management buy-in, was eventually successful.

The issue of management buy-in is central to the success of almost any organization-wide project, and is addressed in many management texts, but of greater relevance here is the variety of systems, processes, negotiations and even names which arose in a single organization. It is a good illustration of decentralization of control, where 'individual lines of business maintain control over the information technology resources necessary to run the applications supporting that line of business' (Loshin, 2011, 60). Loshin notes that a centralized environment, which is what Nestlé finally achieved, reduces duplication and is better suited to data quality control, common usage of metadata and a consistent approach to data quality. However, the centralized environment also means that data quality is only one of the issues which may be competing for attention, and may lose out to operational issues which are seen to be of more immediate importance. Decentralized environments, on the other hand, may focus on data quality issues which impact on a particular line of business, but at the expense of replication of effort, greater drain on resources and ultimate slippage of data standards.

The Nestlé case study is an example of a vertically orientated structure, which had grown up along different product lines and in different geographical divisions. However, we can see, as indeed Nestlé did, advantages in adopting a horizontal approach instead, so that the benefits of good data quality management practices are felt across the organization.

Horizontal versus vertical models

Take the issues addressed in the last chapter, regarding compliance with regulations. If the data from different business processes are segregated in 'silos', then the task of retrieving and integrating them to comply with an information request might be considerable. Suppose, for example, that a customer's details are held on different systems by a marketing department, a sales department, order processing and finance. Suddenly, a Subject Access request could present a challenge which occupies four or more different departmental records, the linkages between which it may be difficult to establish. Even identifying all these instances of data relating to the individual, from the data supplied in the request, could be a problem.

On the positive side, there are incentives to adapt to the horizontal model – where there are different versions of data, the possibility for enrichment exists, and the 'external' data sources with which data can be enriched may actually lie within the same organization. Perhaps the finance department's records have an e-mail address the marketing department could use for an electronic newsletter, or perhaps identifying several customers as members of the same family or household (a process sometimes known as 'householding') could save money spent on duplicate hardcopy mailings, whilst reducing the nuisance factor which might block a sale, because the prospective customers feel swamped.

Enterprise resource planning (ERP) systems, like the SAP system adopted by Nestlé, are a possible answer. Proprietary systems typically consist of a central database, drawn on by modules which are specific to various business functions, such as finance, HR, etc. This would appear to offer a solution to the record duplication problem, but one which might come at the cost of the functionality developed within the vertical systems it replaces. There will also be considerable implications for data conversion and merging. If the new system does not replace the old ones, can they be integrated, and what are the implications there for data quality and other performance metrics?

If we link established systems to a new ERP, Loshin (2011) notes that we may have data conflicts, and also that the ERP's data quality rules may be difficult to integrate, the data formats may be proprietary, rather than open to inspection and integration. There is the alternative of designing 'home-brewed' systems which encapsulate the data quality requirements of the organization, but the skills and funding for systems development may be lacking.

Data quality is increasingly driven by business, and less by IT concerns. Whereas in the past the IT department, or its equivalent, might have voiced concern about data quality, and perhaps have put some data cleansing measures in place, in order to satisfy demands from more than one business department for cleaner incoming data, organizations can now see that there are considerable benefits to be gained from merging data from different sources within the organization – perhaps customer details related to different brands, such as insurance products – and also from outwith the organization – perhaps the NRS survey data mentioned elsewhere. The (conceptually) simple step of merging, checking and deduplicating customer contact details could have a very positive effect on customer loyalty, and hence repeat sales. This is the type of competitive advantage claimed for applying complex and expensive analytic techniques to 'big data', but at a much more affordable cost.

Many organizations acknowledge that there are data quality issues, and that there are silos of data spread across their business which could profitably be merged. A vital first step is a comprehensive data quality assessment, so that you can understand the 'big picture' – not only the issues affecting individual business areas, but perhaps issues affecting the organization more widely. The widely-used 80/20 rule (also known as the Pareto principle) is often held to apply here. It may be that 80% of the problems are due to 20% of the causes, so that there are some 'easy wins' which can be achieved relatively quickly and inexpensively, whereas the longer-term, less dramatic benefits, which potentially require changes to systems rather than to the outputs of the systems, may be better scheduled as part of a longer-term system upgrade plan.

'Easy wins' are a good way of demonstrating the relevance of data quality to business objectives, and of achieving the management-level buy-in which is vital to the success of initiatives of this kind.

Data silos

Having looked at the dimensions of the world of data quality, and some examples of the type of problems which can arise, we must also acknowledge that, even within a single organization, we are likely to be facing multiple instances of these problems, simply because of the ways in which data is handled.

Data 'silos' may emerge in different departments or business units, and may hold variant forms of data, represented differently, stored according to different standards, perhaps conflicting, perhaps simply not recognized as referring to the same entity. There is also a difference between reference data (such as the 'master copy' on your customer file) and transactional data (such as the address the finance department uses for invoicing). Errors in transactional data will tend to have a more immediate, possibly financial, impact, and may therefore tend to attract greater attention, and be fixed more quickly, whereas the central file may not be updated. Historical transactional data is fixed, whereas contact details are subject to change. Customer data is overwhelmingly the data domain regarded as suffering most from poor data quality and/or consistency (Computing, 2013). The 'master copy', of course, is where the data for each transaction should be coming from, and the practice of managing this data, including operations to clean, de-duplicate and enrich it, is known as master data management.

Master data management (MDM)

This is currently a very 'hot topic', but it is simply a restatement of good database practice – there should be one copy of the definitive data, to which all other instances are pointers. Operations – Create, Retrieve, Update, Delete (CRUD) operations – are performed on the definitive copy, and are hence 'cascaded' through the database, or across the organization. Problems arise when departments have their own copies of data, on which they may perform operations with their own systems, and which are not synchronized with a master copy. Another source of problems lies in acquisitions and mergers, when the files of two or more sets of departments may have to be merged. The chances of these being a 'perfect fit' for each other are rather small, and the probability is that work will be needed to merge and deduplicate records. However, each group of original departments will have time and resources invested in operating with their version of the data, so that the implications of undertaking the merger at this level may be significant. However, unless they are faced, more silos will be established, and data integration will move further away.

If MDM can be achieved, then the benefits of all operations on the data are spread across the organization, and only need to be performed once. If we pull in data from the NRS, or correct address data with the postcode database PAF, or enrich with data from social networking sites, then all departments can share the benefits.

Single customer view

As stated above, the domain of customer data suffers most from poor data quality and inconsistency, partly because the 'real-world' entities to which it refers are outwith the control of the organization – they change addresses and names, and they may change suppliers, if not handled carefully. A 'single customer view' is the result of master data management on the files relating to customers. Remember that 'customers' can be internal as well as external to the organization, and that there might not be any financial transactions involved – we're just looking at the entities behind the data, here.

Due to ongoing lack of public confidence in the banking industry, the then UK financial regulator, the Financial Services Authority (FSA), introduced, in 2010, new rules for the Financial Services Compensation Scheme, under which the customers of deposit takers such as banks, building societies and credit unions are compensated in the event of the failure of the deposit taker. Under the new rules, which were intended to ensure that eligible depositors, such as individuals and small businesses, are protected, the FSCS is required to make payments within 20 business days. So that depositors can receive compensation more quickly, the deposit takers are obliged to maintain a single customer view. This has enabled the FSCS to have a pay-out target of seven days, and at worst to stay within the 20-day requirement. From February to July 2011, the FSCS verified reports submitted by deposit takers, and sample data files from those more than 5000 accounts, reporting on its findings to the FSA. The new regulatory body, the

Prudential Regulation Authority, will carry out further work, including further sampling of deposit takers.

Further library examples

As indicated in the introduction to this chapter, we have mainly been referring to databases, and to databases used in all sorts of organizations for all sorts of purposes, though these relate primarily to personal data, because all organizations deal with personal data in some capacity, and personal data are those which are most liable to change. However, all the considerations discussed have relevance, whatever physical or electronic form your 'database' actually takes. At the very simplest end of the continuum, I feel sure that I cannot be the only person who has to reconcile notes from various paper and electronic sources, such as a diary, a personal digital assistant (remember those? – I still have a Palm Pilot), a mobile phone and scribbles on a telephone directory in order to address my Christmas cards each year. That is simply the personal analogue of reconciling your user data.

Staying with formats, how many libraries and other information services have all their records, for all their materials, on a single, up-to-date system? Retrospective conversion of existing records is a major quality issue, because it has a big impact on the accessibility of materials, but it also has significant cost implications.

The variant name problem occurs with user records, of course, but also with names in the catalogue – hence the value of authority files, but the process of reconciling multiple identities to the authority records is one of enrichment.

These operations need to be performed on our existing data, and at the same time, we need to improve our processes, so that further anomalies are kept to a minimum. A lot of the work here is being done by suppliers, by co-operation and networking, but there is still a need to monitor new records for quality and accuracy, whether these originate inside or outside the organization, and to tailor them to specific systems, with holdings records, shelf marks and local notes.

Data quality is an issue for everyone who deals with data, and in some sense, everyone deals with data.

Data quality policy/strategy

> Data quality is more than just a technical issue. It requires senior
> management to treat data as a corporate asset and to realize that the
> value of this asset depends on its quality.
>
> Batini and Scannapieca, 2006, 3

When considering the development of a data quality policy, we need to ask many questions. Are data appropriate, and do they meet users' expectations? Even if they do meet their expectations, are those expectations justified? That is, if you think you have all the genuine data, you'll be happy, but what if you don't? Here, again, there is no substitute for talking to the people who use the data.

In order to begin to answer these questions, it is a very good idea to begin with a data survey. Find out who uses data, and where the same data are used in different organizational functions. In particular, where are different instances of the same data used? We will not refer to these as 'copies', because there is a likelihood that they will not be identical.

There may be several silos, as has been discussed. What we want to do is to approach the 'owners' of each, and involve them in the project. If they can be persuaded, then the right tools for each job can be selected. Probably the same tools will be applicable to more than one job. We need to identify the issues arising from our data survey, and evaluate, across the business, what the impact of the issues is. Remember that some issues may be 'quick fixes' or 'easy wins', while some may be better dealt with alongside longer-term improvements to processes, rather than by (or in addition to) direct manipulation of the data (Computing, 2013).

You need to assess what kind of impact the data issues are having. Is it financial? Does it affect more than one business area? Do you have the resources to handle it yourself, or should you look to outsourcing support to another organization? Would you batch-process (probably existing data) or check on the fly, as new data come in? In library terms, how can we balance the retrospective conversion of existing records with the need to check, correct and possibly create records for new material?

What can you do? Set out minimum requirements for data capture. That sounds quite impressive, but it comes down to providing forms, and encouraging people to complete them properly. If you have buy-in from the 'owners' of the data, reinforced by management, and based on sound financial arguments, that should not be too difficult. People quite like routine, and predictability, and if you can convince them that it cuts down on total workload, that ought to help. Auto-check data input as much as possible. If you have input to a program, try to enforce standards for format and completeness, where possible. If you use web forms, ask the authors to do JavaScript validation of as many fields as possible. However, you will probably want to accept incomplete forms (with a warning) rather than refuse them – incomplete data are better than none at all. If using web forms in conjunction with a database, watch out for SQL injection (the insertion of malicious code into a database) – your web author ought to be able to take precautions which will reject potentially dangerous input. Dates can be authenticated and checked for reasonability. You might also want to think about telephone number formats, for example.

Having acquired data, we should consider storage. In what formats are data stored? In what format are they most useful? Can this be standardized across the organization? Again, this is a matter for discussion, and perhaps negotiation, with the people and departments using the data. An administrative department may want to use readily editable word-processed documents, for example, whilst the legal department may favour portable document format (PDF) images of documents, so that the wording is finalized and images of signatures may be preserved.

The principles which we saw being required in Chapter 2 also make sense in a quality context – the organization should avoid the acquisition of inaccurate, incomplete or outdated data; it should regularly check the quality of the data it holds, not hold them for longer than is necessary and securely delete them at the end of the period where they are useful.

Finally, and always – back-ups! Make absolutely certain that you have a reliable, and tested, back-up procedure in place. Just taking the back-ups is not sufficient – you need to test, and not just once, but regularly, that you can restore from the back-ups you are taking, otherwise they are worse than useless, because having them perpetuates the illusion that your business is protected, whereas in fact it is one slip away from disaster. This issue will come up again in Chapter 5 on security, but it should always be at the forefront of your thinking.

The role of the information professional in data quality management

We have seen in this chapter a range of functions which might fall within the remit of the information professional. The range of materials now extends beyond that which is required for conducting business, and over which there are legal controls, to include day-to-day data, the lifeblood of the organization. The information professional can be a motivator towards significant economies and efficiencies, because the role falls outside the functional arrangement of 'traditional' business departments. By seeing things from a data-related viewpoint, and recognizing that everyone deals with data, we can be instrumental in negotiating the top-level buy-in which is vital to successful change. At all stages of the life-cycle of data, from their creation or acquisition, through use and storage to eventual archiving or disposal, the information professional can provide guidelines and advice.

Practical contributions might include a data review, cleaning up databases to remove redundant entries and enrich definitive ones, designing forms and helping advise programmers or IT staff on requirements and constraints for data input.

....
Discussion points
Think of an organization you work for, or have worked for, or an educational establishment you attend, or have attended. Where might there be data silos? Why might they have arisen? What benefits might be derived from aggregating them?
....

Conclusion

This chapter has discussed the concept of data quality, and described some of the different 'dimensions' of data quality which are commonly identified in the literature. Examples of the adverse effects of poor data quality have been given, and some steps towards remedying these have been discussed. We have also considered the place that improved processes can have in maintaining data quality. Further legal requirements for master data management and a single customer view have added to the external influences on our handling of data, and some practical steps have been discussed. It is important to remember that this is not a one-person issue, but that the role of the information professional encompasses education and encouragement of colleagues towards more effective and efficient working practices.

References

Babbage, C. (1864) *Passages from the Life of a Philosopher,* London, Longman, Green, Longman, Roberts, & Green.

Batini, C. and Scannapieca, M. (2006) *Data Quality: concepts, methodologies and techniques*, Berlin, Springer-Verlag.

Batini, C., Cappiello, C., Francalanci, C. and Maurino, A. (2009) Methodologies for Data Quality Assessment and Improvement, *ACM Computing Surveys*, 41 (3), Article 16 (July 2009), http://doi.acm.org/10.1145/1541880.1541883. [Accessed 05/07/13]

Bovee, M., Srivastava, R. P. and Mak, B. (2001) A Conceptual Framework and Belief-function Approach to Assessing Overall Information Quality, *Proceedings of the Sixth International Conference on Information Quality, Boston, MA, 2001.*

Chisholm, M. (2012) Are the Dimensions of Data Quality Real?, *Information Management*, www.information-management.com/news/are-the-dimensions-of-data-quality-real-10023476-1.html. [Accessed 01/07/13]

Computing (2013) Essential Data Quality: achieving long term success, web seminar. [Accessed 26/07/13]

Dempsey, L. (2013) Names and Identities: looking at Flann O'Brien, Lorcan Dempsey's Weblog, 2 July 2013, http://orweblog.oclc.org/archives/002212.html. [Accessed 02/07/13]

Experian QAS (2013) *Case Study: PDSA*, London.

Financial Services Compensation Scheme (FSCS) (2013) *Single Customer View*, www.fscs.org.uk/industry/single-customer-view. [Accessed 02/08/13]

Gartner (2012) *Magic Quadrant for Data Quality Tools*, https://www.gartner.com/doc/2602515/magic-quadrant-data-quality-tools. [Accessed 05/04/14]

IBM (2009) *Data Quality Management*, http://publib.boulder.ibm.com/infocenter/easrr/v4r2m0/topic/com.ibm.eas.rr.ic.doc/topics/eas_con_dqm.html. [Accessed 01/07/13]

Jarke, M., Jeusfeld, M. A., Quix, C. and Vassiliadis, P. (1999) Architecture and Quality in Data Warehouses: an extended repository approach, *Information Systems*, 24 (3), 229–53.

Loshin, D. (2011) *The Practitioner's Guide to Data Quality Improvement*, Amsterdam, Morgan Kaufmann.

Loshin, D. (2012) *A Data Quality Primer: using data quality tools and techniques to improve business value*, e-book, Melissa Data, www.information-management.com/white_papers/-10024072-1.html. Requires (free) registration. [Accessed 05/04/14]

Madden, N. (2010) Soy-Sauce-Flavored Kit Kats? In Japan, They're No. 1, *AdAge Global*, http://adage.com/article/global-news/marketing-nestle-flavors-kit-kat-japan-markets/142461. [Accessed 16/07/13]

Marks, P. (2009) NASA Criticised for Sticking to Imperial Units, *New Scientist Space*, www.newscientist.com/article/dn17350-nasa-criticised-for-sticking-to-imperial-units.html#.Uf9fhayW60d. [Accessed 05/07/13]

Myers, D. (2013) Dimensions of Data Quality Under the Microscope, *Information Management*, www.information-management.com/news/dimensions-of-data-quality-under-the-microscope-10024529-1.html?portal=data-quality. [Accessed 01/07/13]

Redman, T. (1997) *Data Quality for the Information Age*, Norwood, MA, Artech House, Inc.

Royal Mail Group (2013) *Royal Mail Unveils Improved Access to Postcode Address File*, www.royalmailgroup.com/royal-mail-unveils-improved-access-postcode-address-file. [Accessed 30/07/13]

Sebastian-Coleman, L. (2013) *Managing Data Quality for Ongoing Improvement: a data quality assessment framework*, Amsterdam, Morgan Kaufmann.

Soares, S. (2011) *Selling Information Governance to the Business*, Ketchum, ID, MC Press.

United States Census Bureau (2013) *Hispanic Origin*, www.census.gov/population/hispanic/about/faq.html. [Accessed 03/07/13]

Wand, Y. and Wang, R. Y. (1996) Anchoring Data Quality Dimensions in Ontological Foundations, *Communications of the ACM*, 39 (11), 86–95.

Wang Chao (2012) Swiss Food Tailored for Success, *China Daily USA*, http://usa.chinadaily.com.cn/business/2012-08/20/content_15689213.htm. [Accessed 16/07/13]

Wang, R. Y., Strong, D. and Guarascio, L. M. (1994) *Beyond Accuracy: what data quality means to consumers*, Cambridge, MA, MIT Total Data Quality Management (TDQM) program, http://web.mit.edu/tdqm/www/papers/94/94-10.html. [Accessed 30/07/13]

CHAPTER 4

Dealing with threats

Introduction

Your organization is a custodian of data about your customers, staff and others you do business with, and it is your responsibility to deal with the data in a manner that demonstrates integrity. We have seen, in Chapter 2, that where data protection legislation exists, there is a legal requirement to safeguard personal data. In Chapter 3, we have seen that the data provided by a person in one context may be enhanced or enriched by judicious use of data from other sources. This 'value-added', higher-quality data set is an even bigger asset than what we started with – through synergy it has become more than the sum of its parts and certainly needs the same level of protection.

The Ponemon Institute's eighth annual study into the cost of a data breach in almost 300 companies, nine countries and 16 industries revealed that in 2012, this amounted to an average of US$136 per compromised customer record, a rise from the 2011 figure of US$130 per record (Ponemon Institute, 2013). The costs to German and US organizations, however, were higher, at US$199 and US$188, respectively. Other findings of interest were that data breaches as a result of malicious and criminal attacks and botnets were more costly, and that breaches due to the negligence of insiders accounted for 35% of breaches, malicious attacks being responsible for 37%, and 'system glitches' – IT and business process failures – for the remainder.

There are multiple threats to an organization's data, and the levels of threat behaviour facilitated by the internet, in particular, mean that taking precautions ought to be standard practice, rather than a sign of excessive caution. When an automated scanning program can check millions of IP addresses for vulnerabilities in less time than it takes to describe what it is doing, the responsible way for an organization to act is to erect its defences first, and then build behind them. Prevention rather than cure is what we must aim for, because breaches of security are irreversible, as regards the data that are lost, leaked or damaged.

It has become conventional to divide threats into internal threats, which originate within the organization, and external threats, which come from outside the organization. Although these can have common 'vectors', i.e. use the same media or methods, it is a useful distinction, in that the motivations are largely separable, and different approaches to combating each need to be taken.

Internal threats

If we consider first the notion of a threat as having an aggressive element, the internal threat meeting this description is from the 'disgruntled employee', although ex-employees, particularly recent ex-employees with a grievance, can conveniently be fitted into this category. Silowash et al. (2012) discuss numerous case studies in which 'insiders' – employees who were dismissed from, demoted within or simply left an organization – stole intellectual property (IP), sometimes to take to a new employer, sometimes for sale to other criminals. There are cases of data being deleted, back-ups being tampered with and malicious software installed to damage records after the insider's departure ('logic bombs'). Insiders may not have the technical knowledge and skills often attributed to 'crackers', but the fact that they have privileged access, indeed often more privileged than is strictly necessary for performing their jobs, means that the first hurdle between them and serious data breaches has been at least partly removed. Data can be removed on recordable media, such as CDs or USB sticks, e-mailed or printed off; IP in physical form can be photographed, code can be scrolled and video recorded using a smartphone (another portable data storage device). The growing trend towards homeworking and remote access arguably increases productivity, but also increases opportunity and decreases pressure –

the 'insiders' don't have colleagues watching them (but there may still be automatic logging of user activity). Remember that insiders may be able to set up false accounts, to use existing ones that don't belong to them and to e-mail data to themselves or others. An unauthorized means of gaining access to a system, such as a false account, is sometimes known as a 'back door' – a way in which is not 'forced entry', but is not conventional, and, by implication, is not guarded against.

What can we do? Perhaps as an information professional you will have limited powers in this regard, but part of your function might be to advise on matters regarding threats. If an employee is leaving, change the passwords for any services they have passwords for, look for back doors, and shut off access instantly, particularly if the departure is not amicable. Devise a procedure for handling e-mails addressed to departing and departed employees. Recommend to the HR department that contracts include safeguards relating to data, programs and intellectual property. Recommend credit checks and background checks on prospective employees. Demand that other organizations you're working with meet the same standards for their staff. Work on a minimum knowledge, need-to-know basis. Look at activity for a month prior to and after notification of termination/notice. Recover company property. Set up a security team across the organization, with at least a 'C-level' chair (someone who is 'Chief Security Officer', 'Chief Information Officer', etc.). Do periodic checks, at random, which can also help disguise more targeted checks coming about as a result of tip-offs from within the organization. Encourage a culture where everyone is checking, and everyone is aware of security. Look at people who are working odd or excessive hours, who have financial problems, or who are suddenly well off. If additional access rights are accorded for any reason, remove them immediately that reason has expired. Remove or change passwords on any guest or shared accounts to which they might have had access. Don't have the same person responsible for back-up and restore. Don't keep the offsite back-up in an employee's house – safeguard it properly. Someone's skills and the level of threat they pose are not necessarily commensurate with the position they hold in the organization. Unusual behaviour – anyone boasting about how easy it would be to bring the organization to its knees, or something similar – needs to be watched.

Case study – Bradley Manning

The conviction in August 2013 of Bradley Manning, a US Army Pfc, for multiple charges relating to the biggest leak (through Wikileaks) of classified documents in US history, is an extreme example of an employee breaching security. Manning was acquitted of 'aiding the enemy', but found guilty of:

> multiple other counts, including violations of the Espionage Act, for copying and disseminating classified military field reports, State Department cables, and assessments of detainees held at Guantanamo Bay, Cuba . . . He transmitted the first documents to WikiLeaks in February 2010, sending what came to be known as the Iraq and Afghanistan 'War Logs.' He continued to transmit more material, including a video that showed a U.S. Apache helicopter in Baghdad opening fire on a group of individuals that the crew believed to be insurgents. Among the dead were Iraqi children and two journalists.
>
> Tait (2013)

'Inside outsiders'

It is very important to remember, and this aspect is emphasized by Silowash et al. (2012), that 'insiders' may not belong only to your own organization. In another very high-profile case, Edward Snowden, who leaked US National Security Agency (NSA) documents to Wikileaks, was actually an employee of Booz Allen, a contractor, and not of the NSA itself. Snowden, however, appears to have been one of 1.2 million Americans who had access to that level of material, highlighting the difficulty organizations face in maintaining security (Raywood, 2013). A piece of research conducted in March 2013 by Clearswift, a cyber-security company, found that 83% of UK organizations had 'experienced some form of data security incident in the past year'; 69% of respondents (IT decision-makers in companies of various sizes) saw protection against external threats as a 'key driver' for security, but in fact 58% of the security incidents within their organizations had come from the 'extended enterprise' employees, ex-employees and business partners, compared to 42% originating outside it (Clearswift, 2013).

Acknowledge a big threat

Insiders, unlike intruders, already know where the valuable material is, and one obvious answer to the 'disgruntled employee' scenario is not to have disgruntled employees. Change management is important. It is a wider organizational issue, but the information professional should be sensitive to the working environment, and be aware of potential threats. Make full use of permissions on directories and files, so that information is available on a 'need-to-know' basis only. This may seem a very cloak and dagger or Secret Service approach, but it makes a great deal of sense – staff are exposed only to the information to which they need to have access, and only in the versions and formats they need. This reduces the temptation to explore other areas which do not concern them, and potentially gain access to conflicting versions, outdated information, confidential material or simply material irrelevant to their job. Inevitably, the first iteration of these permissions will need to be corrected, but then changes can be logged, so that there is always a record of who has access to what. Simple awareness that access is traceable may be enough to discourage the opportunist.

Plug the holes

Sending files as e-mail attachments will leave a trace in the e-mail system, but removal of data on removable media such as CDs, DVDs and USB storage devices is harder to stop. It could be a matter of policy to forbid this practice, as we will see later in the chapter, or this threat could be alleviated by removing writing devices and USB ports from corporate computers. Taking this policy to its logical extreme results in the deployment of 'thin clients' – end-user machines which have no hard drives and limited processing power, being effectively terminals attached to a central server, which carries out processing and is connected to storage devices. Thin clients are often used in libraries as catalogue terminals: there is no real justification for providing more than terminal access, and to do so – even having a PC which has to be logged in to the catalogue – is to provide access to temptation to those who might want to exceed their permissions. If someone can log in as a user, there's probably a way for them to log in as staff. If the OPAC belongs to a university library, there may be computer science students using it, and they are notoriously fond of cracking systems. The reputation may be unfair and unjustified, but providing a processor and perhaps a USB port, via which software could be run, might be taking trust in your users a step further than is necessary.

Need to know

In a similar vein, use the facilities of database management systems (DBMS), and this includes integrated library systems, to create appropriate 'views' of databases, so that staff see only the material that is of relevance to their post, and can only change data where they have been granted permission to do so. This protects against accidental, as well as deliberate, misuse. If staff members are cataloguing, they do not need access to circulation functions, and will not be tempted to manipulate their on-loan records, for example. Users should not be able to see each other's loans for privacy and data protection reasons, but also because they might decide to encourage, inappropriately, the return of an item they want to borrow themselves.

Storing a definitive copy of documents on a shared network drive has obvious benefits – everyone with access to the drive can see the same version of the document, if the document's status is 'read-only'. However, if users can edit the document, we need to guard against unauthorized edits. If users take copies of a document, so that they can use it elsewhere, or edit it on their own machines, the problem of different versions arises. Also, there is now the possibility that copies or versions of the document are no longer afforded the limited security they had on the shared drive. If copies are not deleted after use, then there may be security risks. If the provenance of a file on a standalone device is not explicit, out-of-date or potentially damaging data could be accessed by unauthorized users.

Unacceptable behaviour

It is a sad, but unavoidable, fact that when new media are available, some people will use them for unethical purposes. E-mail has been used as a means of bullying, sexual harassment and other forms of behaviour which should not be acceptable in any organization, and there ought to be a workplace policy to forbid this, as will be discussed in the section 'Education about phishing' (see page 108). It is unlikely that employees would use a work e-mail address for spamming, the use of e-mail for inappropriate advertisement of commercial services, but there are other activities, and transmission of types of material, which should be forbidden.

External threats

External threats are the ones that make the headlines. Stories of the latest hacker outrages abound. Personally, I'm of the old school, who think that hacking is something enjoyable and creative – hacking on a program or a piece of hardware is extending its capabilities beyond what it was originally designed to do (Raymond, 2001), and that the activity pursued by malicious individuals or groups is more appropriately known as 'cracking' (Levy, 1984) or simply 'attacking'. However the individuals who engage in the more destructive activities refer to themselves as 'hackers', as do the press and the authorities, so the terminological battle appears to have been lost, and only the 'real' hackers maintain the distinction.

The techniques of crackers are many, as are their skill levels and motivations, and their impact on organizations and individuals is considerable, partly because there is a 'black economy' in cracking tools, and partly because the juvenile, or juvenile-seeming, end of the cracker spectrum exchanges tools freely, and largely untraceably, online. The tools may be pieces of software for activities like 'packet sniffing' or electronic eavesdropping, or password decryption, or may be something as simple as an access code for a proprietary software package. They may also be as dangerous as a kit for building viruses or Trojans – harmful software which we shall be discussing below.

Malware

Software that is intended to harm, or interfere with the operation of, a computer is collectively known as 'malware'. If an electronic hooligan wants a software tool to sniff out passwords from internet traffic, or launch a software worm or virus, or put a Trojan file on a web page which will enslave the computer of anyone downloading it, these are easily available from websites which also disseminate 'warez', or encryption-cracking software. Since there are increasing numbers of these unpleasant pieces of software, with somewhat different characteristics, it is worth looking in slightly more detail at some of the main variants.

Worms

Computer 'worms' first came to widespread public attention in 1988 with the 'Morris worm', so called because it was released by Robert Morris, an American student. Allegedly an attempt to determine the size of the internet at that time, it nevertheless had features designed to conceal its presence, such as camouflaging itself as another program.

Worms are programs which replicate themselves across networks, identifying potential new hosts and infecting them. They may do this by using addresses from an e-mail address book, by scanning the network for servers with vulnerable versions of a particular operating system, or by various other ingenious methods. Being self-replicating, they can rapidly use up memory and storage space on individual computers, leading to crashes, or use up bandwidth on the networks, either simply by the volume of copies being transmitted, or as a result of other actions they are designed to carry out. For example, one worm, Code Red, was designed in such a way as to launch simultaneous requests from all its instances to the White House server in the USA, a strategy which would have brought down the server had remedial action (a temporary change in the server's address) not been undertaken. Their varying methods of replication mean that worms are spread by different methods, so that there is no single way of avoiding infection. Some of the most widespread instances of infection have been via e-mails which encourage users to open an attachment, the infamous 'ILOVEYOU' worm of 2000 being an example. An e-mail with that subject line carried as an attachment a Visual Basic script (a virus) which, on being activated by opening, forwarded the e-mail to the first 50 addresses in the Microsoft Outlook address book on the affected computer. Since the addresses came from the address book, the e-mails were more likely to be trusted by the recipients, increasing the likelihood of spread, enhanced by the personal nature of the subject line and the attachment, which purported to be a love letter. This is an example of 'social engineering', which we shall encounter again later. This script renamed certain media files on the infected computer, but its main impact was as a time-waster, because of the effort involved in removing it.

In 2004 the Sasser worm, which spread by scanning network ports on network-connected machines, and then exploiting a security hole in the Windows operating system to cause a 'buffer overrun', swamped systems in many organizations, including a French press agency, a Finnish bank, the British Coastguard, Deutsche Post and the European Commission.

The Conficker virus in 2009 infected millions of Windows computers, apparently turning them into a 'botnet' – a group of computers, under the direction of an attacker, acting without their owners' knowledge – which could attack financial institutions. Although many PCs are still infected, the botnet does not appear to have been activated (Weinberger, 2012).

Worms can potentially have much more serious effects – the 'payload' of malicious programming they carry can be extremely harmful. It is largely due to the huge expansion in the use of anti-virus and related software that extremely harmful instances are not much greater in number.

So, what might be termed worms' more 'attention-getting' activities are less of a threat currently, partly because of the ability of security software to detect them. A more insidious use of worms is not directly related to the replication and spreading, but to their role in the delivery of payloads, which can include other forms of malicious programming, such as viruses.

Viruses

Viruses are small programs which typically cause damage to your system. They can conceal themselves in other files, and are often disguised as e-mail attachments, presented in such a way as to entice people to open them. For example, they may appear to be electronic greetings cards, or links to sites where you are told a card will be available, but which in fact will infect your machine. They may appear to be images, programs or documents. They may be acquired when downloading files from websites, and are particularly likely to be acquired from sites which are themselves of a 'dubious' nature, such as those hosting pornographic or cracking-related material, or pirated software (warez sites). They can corrupt files, erase disks, and spread to other computers. They may have the effect of 'hijacking' a computer, perhaps without its user's knowledge, to perform illegal activities, as we shall see later.

In 2013, a Microsoft Technet blog post reported on a pair of viruses, Vobfus and Beebone, which work together. Vobfus is transmitted on removable media, including USB sticks and removable drives, and on mapped network drives. Once established, it contacts a 'command and control' (C&C) centre, and downloads Beebone, whilst itself infecting other connected drives. Beebone contacts the C&C centre and downloads URLs from which it downloads other malware, and it also downloads other versions of Vobfus. Because of this co-operative action, the infections are very hard to deal with (Choi, 2013).

Viruses have also had an impact in the physical world. In 2009–2010, the Stuxnet virus did a large amount of damage to Iranian nuclear processing plants, by causing their centrifuges to spin out of control and self-destruct (Weinberger, 2012).

As can be seen from the examples, the distinction between the viruses which do the damage and the worms used to spread them is a fine one, and not easy to make. It comes down to technicalities, and particular specimens are identified as viruses or worms partly on the basis of which aspect of their behaviour is under discussion. It is not particularly helpful to nit-pick about which is which, and we shall see that the measures which we need to put in place to defend our systems are common to both. It is also worth noting that a lot of the inconvenience caused by worms, viruses and Trojans is indirect – it is due to the number of (frequently exaggerated, but usually well intentioned) e-mails which are sent warning about them. Sometimes, these threats only manifest as a bandwidth-sapping stream of e-mails.

Trojans

Trojans, or Trojan horse programs, operate in a different way to worms and viruses. They do not replicate, or spread from computer to computer. A computer infected by a Trojan might log keystrokes, such as logins and passwords, and pass them back to its owner, or it might make the host machine part of a 'botnet', to be used in a DDoS attack, discussed below. The name comes from the story of the Trojan horse in Virgil's *Aeneid*, in which the Greek besiegers of Troy left a large wooden horse outside the city gates, and withdrew. Supposing the horse to be a gift, the citizens brought it inside the city gates, but at night Greek soldiers climbed out of the hollow horse, opened the city gates, and thus brought the siege to an end.

Trojans masquerade as useful or desirable programs or files. They look as if they are useful (perhaps claiming to make your system run faster), but actually they take control of the system, though this may not be obvious to the user – an apparent slowing of the system may be the only noticeable sign. Trojans may be installed as part of a program, particularly one installed from a less-than-reputable site, while playing an online game or other internet application, or as a so-called 'drive-by download', where the user is encouraged to click on a prompt, perhaps ostensibly to dismiss a pop-up window, but in fact prompting a concealed download of the malware.

Fake system security software and fake system optimization programs are a popular way of delivering malware. These offers will often appear in a pop-up window when someone visits an infected site, offering to scan your system to make it run faster, or to rid it of a virus which the advertisement claims has been detected on your system. A bit of consideration should lead you to conclude that this is not how a reputable organization would market its products, but unfortunately, the fear of a security threat, and the promise of a quick fix, is enough to make many people allow the program to run. Ironically, of course, the promised 'fix' is itself a threat, in many cases.

Trojans can 'recruit' your computer as part of a botnet, send their 'owner' data such as credit card details and passwords or install other malware – the possibilities are practically unlimited, because what has happened is that unauthorized software has been allowed to run on the computer, so its operations are really only circumscribed by the fact that Trojans are probably more useful to their creator while they remain undiscovered. They may be discovered by others, though – malware can run a 'port scan' on a network, and identify machines which have been compromised by a Trojan, and proceed to add them to a botnet, for example.

The first commercial Trojan program targeted at Linux users appeared in 2013 (Vaughan-Nichols, 2013). Linux is inherently more secure than Windows, so the Trojan can only be delivered by running malicious programs, or visiting malicious websites; but not clicking on URLs you cannot identify in e-mails, for example, is another subject for user education.

Trojans can be targeted as phishing e-mails towards a particular organization – see 'Phishing' (page 94). Another way of reaching particular groups of users is through the 'watering hole' attack, named for a strategy used by predators in the wild, where prey animals in arid regions can dependably be found in the vicinity of watering holes. In a 'watering hole' attack, a website of interest to a particular demographic, such as programmers using a particular programming language, will be compromised or faked, and booby-trapped with malware.

Spyware

Spyware could be considered as a sub-class of Trojans. This is software which installs itself on a computer, with the objective of monitoring and reporting back activity, often for advertising purposes. Although the operations of the spyware may be limited to logging websites visited, or reading 'cookies' – the small pieces of code often left on a computer by websites which have been visited – it may also monitor keystrokes, record and transmit credit card numbers and passwords, and look at other data on the computer. In fact, the potential activities of spyware are as wide as those of other Trojan software, and it is distinguished primarily by the fact that its purpose is to gather information to be used for, or sold to be used for, advertising purposes.

Rootkits

Another variant on the Trojan theme, and probably the most difficult to deal with, rootkits can actually do what a lot of the scaremongering messages about viruses and Trojans claim – they really take over the infected computer. The name comes about because in Unix-like operating systems, the administrator account with most privileges is called the 'root' account. The 'kit' part just signifies the fact that these pieces of malware are tools, assembled to serve a particular function.

A rootkit loads itself into the computer's memory at boot time, 'below' the operating system, which is therefore unaware of the rootkit's presence, as the rootkit is able to rewrite the internal memory map to conceal its own existence. It can also conceal the presence of other programs, which may themselves be malware. Once the rootkit is in place, the system is more or less at its mercy, and detection is difficult, because the system cannot 'see' it.

Denial of service attacks

A 'botnet' is a large number (it could be in the tens of thousands) of machines which have been infected, unknown to their actual owners, and can be used by the cracker to carry out large-scale attacks, often of the type characterized as 'distributed denial of service' (DDoS). The term 'distributed' refers to the geographically distributed machines in the 'botnet', and the attack is a more sophisticated version of the older denial of service (DoS) attack, which employed fewer machines.

A DDoS attack simply takes advantage of the client/server architecture on which the world wide web is based, to overwhelm the capacity of a server to respond to requests for files, by making a number of requests so great that the target server cannot respond. This has the effect of shutting down a website, because the availability of a site online lies simply in the server's ability to send files to those who send it requests. These attacks are typically costly in terms of lost revenue, and perhaps lost reputation, but are not physically damaging to computer systems, although they may cause system resets. It is theoretically possible that physical damage can be caused by the attack opening an avenue to 'flash' updates of firmware, rendering physical damage to devices such as routers or printers, but this does not appear to be observed 'in the wild'; however, the attacks can facilitate the invasion of systems by malware.

Denial of service attacks are difficult to defend against, because the traffic is difficult to distinguish from legitimate traffic and difficult to block whilst still allowing legitimate traffic through. There are claimed software solutions: however, the fact that 'hacktivists' such as the Anonymous group can bring off DDoS attacks on very large corporations, which might be assumed to have such protection in place, leads to the conclusion that the most pragmatic approach is to prepare for the worst – to look at the scenario not 'if', but 'when', an attack takes place. These attacks are attacks on capacity, whether on bandwidth or processing capability, and the most successful strategy would appear to be one of overprovision in both areas. This would mean arranging with your service provider and your hardware provider for a peak capacity many times in excess of what you might expect as a result of normal business traffic. It is possible that arrangements can be made for such capacity to be 'swapped in' on demand.

A newer solution involves cloud technology – traffic constituting a suspected DDoS attack is rerouted via the cloud, where it is scanned, and the 'bad' packets are filtered out. This is, of course, a commercial solution, and comes at a cost, but may be worth exploring, given the potential costs of a successful attack.

Phishing

'Phishing' is a very common forerunner to fraud, so-called because an attacker is 'fishing' for your personal information. It is most often encountered as e-mail, in which someone purporting to be your IT department, bank, building society, tax office, PayPal or other organization, encourages you to visit a website, where you will be prompted to enter your login and/or account details. The reason given for this may be 'so that your account can be verified', or because 'unusual activity has been detected on your account', or because your mailbox size has been exceeded, or some other plausible-seeming excuse. The official-looking website will be a spoof, designed simply to capture your details. It may have design flaws which would give it away, or there may be something suspicious about the URL, but these sites are increasingly sophisticated. A first step towards combating phishing is to discount e-mails from banks with which you do not have an account, tax offices from which you do not expect a rebate, lotteries you have not entered, friends you don't actually know, and any surviving relatives of recently deceased and wealthy overseas figures, who need to move money out of their country and will pay you a premium. Once these are disposed of, if there are any you are sure are genuine, contact the apparent sender, *but not by replying to the e-mail, or using any links or contact details in the e-mail.*

Phishing is not just a threat to the individual, though that's the aspect we perhaps tend to think of – someone obtains your login details, so they can do something bad. We have to remember that these are login details to a service, which is provided by an organization, and that this, probably ill-intentioned, person now has some level of privileged access which they did not have before. The level, of course, depends on whose details they are using, but it certainly gives them more leverage than they had previously. We are not primarily concerned here with the threat to the individual, who may have their own account compromised, but to the organization, which has had a path opened through its security. There is also a wider concern, in that the publicity given to successful breaches of security, through phishing or other means, devalues the public's trust in the safety of using this type of service (for example, online banking, where phishing attempts are rife), even though the online service is inherently more secure than its paper- and mail-based counterparts (Abourrous et al., 2010).

Bank mergers, financial uncertainty and, in the UK, the confusion over reclaiming payment protection insurance on mortgages (PPI) are all fostering an environment in which phishing can flourish, simply because of people's uncertainty as to which bank they're with, what businesses are legitimate and what they should reveal.

Case study – security awareness in a bank

Abourrous et al. (2010) conducted a series of tests using phishing techniques against bank personnel. A telephone approach, using social engineering techniques (see next section), persuaded 32% of the subjects to reveal their user names and passwords. An e-mail plus fake website approach fooled 44% into supplying their actual credentials. A test whereby the subjects were asked to discriminate between fake and genuine websites discovered 72% misidentification among staff who had not received training in recognizing phishing techniques. Amongst the trained group, however, 72% of decisions were correct. So, although training would appear to be beneficial, there are still significant numbers of wrong decisions, and the figures are more alarming because it might be thought that bank staff (and IT staff were among those deceived) would be more cautious than average users about such lapses in security.

Social engineering

Despite warnings, people will still reveal their login details, under the impression that the request comes from their own IT department, or their own bank – the very people who don't have to ask, because they administer them. Exploitation of users' good faith by pretending to have the authority to ask for their login or other details, or in general obtaining sensitive information from people, rather than from computers, is known as 'social engineering'.

Black hats and white hats

Some vulnerabilities arise through poor coding of software, perhaps a program using a web input form which allows SQL injection (the insertion of malicious code into a database). Some may arise from so-called 'zero-day exploits'. An 'exploit' is a security hole in a program, which may be exploited by an attacker (good grammar is not valued highly amongst crackers). Some of these weaknesses are made public, so that attackers can use them before the software publisher has a chance to rectify the situation – the attack occurring on 'day zero' of awareness of the flaw (numbering in programming conventionally begins from zero, as in 0, 1, 2, 3, 4 . . .). Getting code checked and fixed is a possibility, and there are 'white-hat hackers' in the form of security consultants, who can be employed to do 'penetration testing'. (The colour of the hat is an allusion to old Western movies, in which the 'goodies' wore white Stetsons, and the 'baddies' black ones.) 'Black-hat hackers' are the bad guys – the socially irresponsible, or downright criminal, individuals and groups who break into systems, often with the intent of doing damage. In their own eyes, their motivation is often described as curiosity, rather than malice or profit, and it sometimes happens that 'black hats' who are caught and prosecuted, reinvent themselves as 'white hats'; or security consultants.

Case study – Kevin Mitnick

One of the best-known instances of this change of direction was that of Kevin Mitnick, the subject of several books and many articles, who was at one time in the 1980s the most wanted computer criminal in the USA (Hafner and Markoff, 1995) and now runs Mitnick Security Consulting, LLC. Mitnick served five years in prison, and was released under supervision for a further three years, during which his online activities were curtailed. His original offence was theft of software from Digital Equipment Corporation (DEC), and while on supervised release after a one-year prison sentence for that offence, he committed numerous offences against cell-phone providers, and went 'on the run'. It would appear, though, that Mitnick's talents lay primarily in 'social engineering' rather than in advanced computing skills, and the books he has published since the end of a ban on him profiting from publications about his activities reinforce this (Mitnick, 2002; Mitnick, 2005). Mitnick found that simply telephoning workers and pretending to be from the IT department of their company can result in many of them disclosing password details. In a video interview (Kerner, 2013), Mitnick also explains that innocently opening e-mail attachments can be a major source of problems, because of the payload they can conceal.

The unwitting internal threat

It is very important to recognize that an organization's own staff may be acting in a manner which is tantamount to inviting intrusion into the organization's systems, although they are quite ignorant of the fact. Since the advent of Myspace, Bebo and Facebook around 2003, social networking has seen an explosive rise in participation. In addition to this, it has added to the original social uses a quite respectable work/professional aspect, with sites like LinkedIn promoting professional networking, organizations doing business through Facebook pages, YouTube becoming a means of income or supplementary income for many, and so on. Sawyer (2013) presents a worrying set of scenarios, in which innocent (and unconscious) information sharing opens up potential for abuse. Because of the social origins of the sites, many of us feel that these are social spaces, and carry on conversations with friends as we might do face to face. This might include things like moaning about your job, posting a picture of you and your colleagues in the office, telling everyone how many days are left until your holidays, or posting pictures of your children, pets (especially cats) and significant other[s]. So far, so good, but now think of these posts from the viewpoint of a social engineer. If you complain about your job, maybe you're unhappy there, and you might be less guarded about security. Photos of your colleagues show who they are, how closely you work together, and could be combined with other information, perhaps from a company website, or from LinkedIn, to build a fuller picture of you and your workplace. Simply who your 'friends' are says a lot about you, as the saying goes – it's an old expression, but as regards your online identity, it could hardly be more apposite. Digital photos are often tagged with metadata, such as date, time, and sometimes geolocation, all of which could be useful – there may be circumstances where your organization may not wish to publicize the location of all its premises, but the metadata can give it away.

These were examples of the potential leaks of work-related material into a social 'space'. Social networking applications can also expose to exploitation leakage of social material into a work space. It is well known that, despite constant warnings to the contrary, otherwise intelligent people will use as passwords the names of spouses, children, loved ones or pets, vehicle registrations, names or other details of sports teams, and other words which are easily associated with the individual by those who know them. If the person guessing the password knows you well, the outcome might not be more serious than 'fraping' – the 'humorous' posting left by someone else accessing a Facebook account. However, this kind of information is often now made available to the world by those who do not pay attention to their privacy settings on social networking sites.

Another consequence of this leakage of the private into the public arena also concerns passwords, this time to online services. Almost any service that requires a login user name and password has helpful links to turn to if you forget one or the other, often both. Sometimes, a forgotten password will simply be mailed to the e-mail address from which you opened your account. Given people's tendency to use the same password for multiple accounts, this is a bad thing – someone with access to your e-mail account (which may also have the same password, of course) could potentially access all those services. Some sites, however, take the additional step of asking you to answer a 'security' question to which you've already provided the answer, and to which only you could supposedly know the answer. These questions tend to be very similar, and the answers include: your mother's maiden name, the name of your first school, the name of your first pet, a favourite place to go on holiday, or the model of your first car – just the kind of information, in fact, that people post on social networking sites.

It is also wise to remember that the kind of information you are encouraged to post (favourite books, films, etc.), the groups you join and the friends you have (and you do actually know all those people, don't you?) are very much the kind of information a social engineer could use to work their way into your confidence, and perhaps your account.

We have to remind users that work and social lives should be separate, and that the same security considerations which they would be well advised to apply to their personal online lives are also important from a work perspective. If an employee has a high-profile online persona, which publicly identifies them as an employee of the organization, it is incumbent upon them to behave in a manner which does not bring the organization into disrepute. That is a reasonably uncontroversial position for the organization to take, and we should make the most of the opportunity presented by reminding employees of this (see 'Education about social networking' on page 105) to reinforce good personal 'information hygiene' practices.

The law

Unsurprisingly, legislation has struggled to keep pace with developments in the field of data threats. In the UK, the Computer Misuse Act 1990 defined the offences of:

1 Knowingly using a computer to gain unauthorized access to 'any program or data held in any computer'.
2 Unauthorized access (as in 1) with intent to commit or facilitate commission of further offences.
3 Knowingly performing unauthorized acts with intent to impair a computer or its programs or data.

On a much broader scale, the Council of Europe Convention on Cybercrime, 2001 has been ratified by 39 states, and signed but not ratified, by another 12. 'Ratification' in this context means that a state establishes its consent to be bound by a treaty, for example by passing legislation, rather than simply declaring its intention not to work against the treaty. The ratifying states who are not members of the Council of Europe are Australia, Japan, the Dominican Republic and the USA.

In the USA, the Computer Crime and Intellectual Property section of the Department of Justice (DoJ) works to prevent, investigate and prosecute computer and intellectual property crime both domestically and internationally. The USA has more than 40 Federal statutes relating to the prosecution of computer-related crimes, which the DoJ divides into those concerning the acquisition of hardware and software illegally; those directly targeting networks and computers (e.g. distributing viruses and Trojans); and those committed through the use of computers and networks, such as fraud, identity theft and intellectual property infringement.

One of the main pieces of legislation used in prosecutions has been

18 USC 1030, the Computer Fraud and Abuse Act, originally enacted in 1986, although subject to frequent amendments since then, notably the USA Patriot Act in 2002 and the Identity Theft Enforcement and Restitution Act in 2008 (Doyle, 2010). Originally intended to cover classified information held on government computer systems, the reach of this law has gradually been extended by Congress, and the decision in 1996 that it should include in its definition of 'protected' computers those 'used in interstate or foreign communications', has effectively broadened its scope to any computer with an internet connection, smartphones and tablets.

Additionally, many US states have followed the lead of California, and have made it mandatory to report to the authorities any security breaches involving exposure of personal information. In the UK:

> [a]lthough there is no legal obligation on data controllers to report breaches of security which result in loss, release or corruption of personal data, the Information Commissioner believes serious breaches should be brought to the attention of his Office. The nature of the breach or loss can then be considered together with whether the data controller is properly meeting his responsibilities under the DPA.
>
> Information Commissioner's Office (2012)

The reappearance of the ICO should serve to remind us that the implications of data loss, release or corruption can go beyond direct inconvenience or cost to the organization – failure of a data controller to meet its responsibilities can have its own penalties, in financial and reputational senses.

Policy

This is an area where the issues are quite clear-cut, and the measures which should be put in place are well understood by many information professionals. Unfortunately, the practice of defending against threats to your data is undeniably not one of the more exciting areas of the job. However, the level of threat is such that systems with an internet connection will undoubtedly be attacked at some point.

It ought to be obvious, but . . .

Keep back-ups. Of course, this should be second nature to information professionals, but, of course, it only becomes so after either a major loss of work or a very 'close shave'. Silos are a problem here, too. If a department is using its own systems, with its own copies of data, are these subject to the organization-wide back-up policy which ought to be in place? This issue will also appear under the heading 'Back-ups' in the next chapter (see page 128), but remember that data which is not backed up properly is a threat which is as yet unresolved.

Change default login and password settings for network devices such as routers and switches – lots of these are left at factory settings, and it doesn't require any special cracking skills to find out what these are, because lists are easily accessible on the internet.

Temporary and guest accounts are often set up for specific events, after which they may be forgotten, until they are reactivated by someone who may have bad intentions. Accounts which are set up on an ad hoc basis, perhaps under time pressure, perhaps to cater for an urgent request for guest access, may not have been optimally configured from a security point of view, and may escape deletion, precisely because they are out of the ordinary, and do not come under any regular 'housekeeping' schedule.

Firewalls and anti-virus software

The defence proper should start with a firewall. A firewall, implemented in software or hardware, examines packets of data entering and leaving a system, and blocks those which should not be allowed through, based on a system of internal rules. Firewalls range in sophistication and complexity from those packaged with operating systems, (e.g. Windows Firewall) through highly configurable software solutions to hardware-based solutions which maintain a 'demilitarized zone' (DMZ) between an organizational network and the external network environment.

A firewall can guard against suspicious incoming packets, but why would you need to check outgoing packets? Some malware may have got past your firewall, or you may have inadvertently installed it by running a program from a download, or surfing an infected website, or opening an attachment in an e-mail, or by any of the other infection vectors which your firewall cannot detect, or is not updated to detect. Updating firewall software is probably more important than updating any other software, except for patches dealing with known security issues. Some malware is equipped with the ability to 'phone home' – to send a message to its originator, which may be a confirmation that your computer has now become part of a botnet, or may contain a payload such as your contacts list from your e-mails, your credit card details from logging your keystrokes (looking for a pattern of 16 numbers, then three for the security code, for example) or anything else on your computer that looks interesting to the owner.

Anti-virus programs are widely available, including some free ones that are quite well regarded, and Windows itself has Microsoft Security Essentials built-in, so there is really no excuse for not using one. However, they must be kept updated with the latest virus 'signatures' – distinctive pieces of code which the anti-virus software can identify – frequently. Usually, this can be done online, and automatically. The software should then be able to stop some attempts to download harmful software onto a machine, and should be able to carry out scans for malicious software already in place, or of new files which can be scanned 'on demand'. Remember, though, that even when updated, antivirus software will always be one step behind the virus authors – it can only detect threats it knows about, and this will only be after their presence has been detected by their appearance 'in the wild', usually at some cost to a victim. Use of antivirus software is no substitute for practising good information hygiene, as recommended under 'Education about social networking' (see page 105).

Patches and updates

Guard your website against hosting malware – keep patches up to date, and run daily scans. Guard against hosting malicious advertisements – this could cause search engines to block your site, which could greatly damage your revenues and reputation. Ensure your SSL certificates – digital certificates which guarantee the authenticity of your site – are up to date.

Lots of libraries have public access web machines – these need to be checked, perhaps on a daily basis.

Software patches must be kept up to date – an article by Greenberg (2013) explains that Lily Collins has become the most dangerous celebrity to search for on the internet, because of the frequency with which such searches led to sites with malware: 'unwary fans can be compromised in any number of ways by clicking risky links, downloading images and videos, or downloading media players or updates. Those who have forgone updates and patches run the risk of being infected in a 'drive-by' fashion without ever knowingly downloading a thing'.

Passwords

If someone has physical access to your computer, your security is compromised. You can, and should, set passwords on your account, and lock your screen when away from the computer, but, given a little time, an attacker can get access to your account.

Having established physical security, we need to look at policies regarding passwords. Passwords are in any case fraught with problems.

Passwords which can be found in a dictionary don't work – they can be cracked by a 'brute force' approach, which simply involves trying all the words in a dictionary. A computer can do this very quickly, even more so if the attacker has access to the encrypted form of the password, which they can often get on a Unix-based system, in the '/etc/passwd' file. Although the encryption algorithm (the process by which the plain-text password is encrypted) may be very hard to reverse (the attacker can't easily get from the encrypted form to the plain-text form), all that needs to be done is to encrypt all the words in the dictionary, and record those which match the encrypted password you have. If the attacker has copied the whole 'passwd' file, which would be a reasonable assumption, then the chances of them finding a match are much improved.

If passwords are 'strong' – at least eight characters of mixed upper and lower case letters, symbols and numbers – they are also harder to remember, especially if, as is also recommended, you use a different password for each site and application, change them frequently, and don't record them anywhere. Names of pets and partners, car registrations, pets' names and names and dates of birth of family members are all worth exploring for the curious cracker, and much of this information is readily available from social networking sites or simple web searches.

There are network administration tools which prompt users to renew their password regularly, some of which will also test password 'strength', and block the re-use of previously used passwords. Using these tools, when available, is a good idea. It is preferable, where possible, to give the user a small number of logins before they are forced to change the password, as a password chosen in haste is unlikely to be either secure or memorable.

There are programs which generate 'strong' passwords, there are programs and online services which will store all your passwords, supplying them on demand from an encrypted 'vault' on your own computer, or from a website, on production of a master password, which is the only one you need remember.

Some browsers offer to store passwords that you have asked them to remember, but they can be found by those who know how to reveal them or can search for the technique on a search engine. 'Show X saved passwords' is a good start, where 'X' is the name of the browser. Internet Explorer does have a small authentication process to complete, but this is not a serious hindrance to the attacker. Unless you are the only person who has access to your computer, this is not a feature that it is advisable to use. Similar features, which offer to 'auto-fill' your address, e-mail and credit card details into forms, should also be treated with extreme caution.

Education about social networking

Social networking on sites like Twitter and Facebook (or whatever the hot one is this week) is amazingly widespread. The sites are routinely used by prospective employers to vet applicants, and by current employers to monitor current employees, or at least to monitor what people are saying about their organization, and some of these people might be current employees. This is not the best place to debate whether this approach by the employer is a good thing or not, but employees should be reminded that their activities on social media forums are public, and that bringing their employer into disrepute would be unprofessional. This would also be an opportune time to re-emphasize the importance of good practice regarding passwords, stressing in particular that the use of work login details in social sites is absolutely forbidden. A policy about social networking needn't be very restrictive, but having a policy means you have something to point to, and something the staff have signed up to, which might be very useful if things come to a head for some reason.

Education about e-mail

Educate your users, as far as possible, about the dangers of clicking on links in e-mails, or opening e-mail attachments. Attachments do not have to be executable (program) files to do damage – Office documents can conceal 'macros', which are effectively small programs that run when the file is opened, Portable Document Format (PDF) files can conceal functional code and files which are displayed by your e-mail program as having a harmless-looking extension may have a .exe extension appended to that, which is simply not displayed by the mail program – there are many ways in which you can be tricked into running a program. Once you do, the program runs with your permissions: if you as a user have permissions to read, write, execute, delete or install files and programs, so do the programs you run, irrespective of whether you realize you are running them. This is one of the reasons why, even if you have the use of an administrative account, or a 'superuser' account, such as 'root' on Unix-like systems, it is important that you use it only for administrative functions, and revert to your normal user account for everything else – it is too easy to forget that you are operating with extra privileges, and to accidentally do something harmful and irrevocable.

When you innocently run that malicious program concealed in your e-mail, you are effectively logging the attacker into your system, with your privileges. When you click on the link in Facebook to the film called 'Teenager prays her parents never see this film' which, rather uncharacteristically, appears to have been posted by one of your normally conservative friends (oddly, it doesn't display – 'link must be broken') – you're welcoming the attacker in. Perhaps luckily for you, although not for your system, the attackers have their sights set on actions more profitable than just trashing your files. If your computer can be secretly made part of a botnet, then it can effectively be rented out for use in criminal activities. Also, you probably have an e-mail account with addresses of friends and colleagues, who might be more likely to open an attachment in an e-mail that appears to come from you, because you're trustworthy and wouldn't send them anything dangerous – and so it goes on.

Education about Trojans

Trojans are the form of malware which it is most within our capability to avoid. Worms and viruses are more-or-less autonomous. They might be triggered by opening an e-mail, but we can't really stop people opening all e-mails, though we can ask them to consider very carefully which ones they open. Trojans, however, need to pull on us the trick after which they're named, so we have to be extra cautious.

Don't use the preview features in applications like Microsoft Outlook e-mail. These are opening files for you, without even giving you the chance to decide that they might be suspect.

Downloading files is like opening the city gates and bringing in the horse. You certainly shouldn't download files from people or from websites unless you have good reason to trust them, and even if you do, you should still scan the file with an anti-virus program. Because Trojans can be spread to someone's address book, be very cautious about friends sending files you didn't ask for, or attached to a message which doesn't otherwise refer to them. It doesn't take long to check with the friend.

Are the filenames what they appear to be? Windows' default settings are often to display only the first extension of a filename, perhaps concealing from you the '.exe' on the end, which might give it away as an executable, potentially malicious, program. Set your view options in your file manager program (such as Windows Explorer) to show all filename extensions. Don't download and execute files to try them out (irchelp.org, 2012).

Education about phishing

'If it seems to be too good to be true, it probably is'; 'Freebies are worth what you pay for them'; 'There ain't no such thing as a free lunch'. Plenty of folk wisdom tells us that phishing-type approaches are suspect. Getting this across without appearing to patronize your colleagues may be tricky, so you may as well cover chain-letter e-mails, the fake virus alert alarmist bandwidth-clogging e-mails, and physical enhancement offers at the same time. That way, everyone has some other gullibility to laugh at, and with luck will quietly note that their own is on a par with it.

Education about social engineering

As well as warning people about social engineering, which will be only partially effective, because people are unwilling to admit, even to themselves, that they could easily be fooled, you can at least reduce the risk of any internal part of your organization being impersonated in a social engineering attempt. Adopt, enforce and, most of all, publicize the policy that no one will ever be asked for their system or network password. The only people who could have a legitimate reason for asking for your password, in that they might want to test logging in as you, would be the IT department. Anyone else could, and should, go through the IT department. The IT department can reset your password, so don't need to know what it is. Remember, and get your colleagues to remember: the important thing is not who is calling you, it's what they're asking you for.

Acceptable use policies (AUP)

As discussed above, certain types of behaviour are unacceptable within the organization, and employees should be required to sign up to an acceptable use policy in order to protect people from the consequences of such behaviour, and to protect the organization from the consequences of such behaviour being carried out using their equipment and connectivity. The JANET Acceptable Use Policy (Wood, 2011) is intended primarily for academic institutions, but is a good template on which an AUP could be based.

Hardware

One vector of threats to an organization's security is via the use of hardware. Storage devices, such as CDs, DVDs and USB devices, can be used for moving data into and out of the organization without leaving behind the electronic traces caused by downloading files to, or uploading files from, a user's account, or by receiving or sending them via e-mails.

As noted above, this is a channel which could be used either to introduce potentially harmful material (programs, or files infected with viruses, etc.) or to remove data, programs or other intellectual property. It is worth considering implementing a policy which bans these devices from the workplace, and it should also be considered whether CD and DVD-writing drives should be installed on corporate machines. Depending on the nature of 'at-risk' information, it might be considered wise to restrict the use of scanners as well, though banning removable storage devices restricts the potential for removing scanned image files.

The organization might consider adopting a policy on Bring Your Own Device (BYOD) – a practice which has taken off with the proliferation of smartphones, tablet computers and wireless networking (see page 150). All of these devices can be used for data storage, and can be connected wirelessly to networks.

This potential problem will be considered again in Chapter 5.

· ·
Exercise

Workplace posters are a good, non-confrontational way of getting information across. Design a poster, or a series of posters, explaining how to avoid viruses, worms and Trojans.
· ·

Conclusion

In this chapter, we have looked at areas which are potentially very sensitive, not only because of the material which might be under threat, though that is certainly a major consideration, but because the nature of threats and the means of controlling them impact on people's working practices and indeed on their daily lives.

Many of the issues considered above can be remedied through education, as the section on policy has described. However, it is very important that this is delivered properly. If people feel that they are being patronized, or mocked for their ignorance, they are more likely to rebel against any advice than to comply with it. It is also important to remember that we are discussing very new technologies and even newer threats, which have arisen long after much of the workforce may have gained their computer experience. Those who do not deal with computers with an eye to security may quite legitimately be unaware of much of the material in this chapter, so education must be done with sensitivity.

The huge range of threats can seem overwhelming, but it is important to remember that the steps to reduce or eliminate the threats are individually quite simple. Make your policy clear, explain the reasons for all elements of the policy, and ensure that it is applied fairly and equitably. If there are exceptions, explain why.

References

Abourrous, M. R., Hossain, M. A., Dahal, K. P. and Thabatah, F. F. (2010) Experimental Case Studies for Investigating E-Banking Phishing Techniques and Attack Strategies, *Journal of Cognitive Computation*, 2 (3), 242–53. DOI: 10.1007/s12559-010-9042-7.

Choi, H. (2013) *Viewing Vobfus Infections From Above*, Microsoft Malware Protection Center, http://blogs.technet.com/b/mmpc/archive/2013/06/30/viewing-vobfus-infections-from-above.aspx. [Accessed 05/09/13]

Clearswift (2013) *The Enemy Within Research 2013*, www.clearswift.com/about-us/pr/press-releases/enemy-within-research-2013. [Accessed 18/09/13]

Doyle, C. (2010) *Cybercrime: a sketch of 18 USC 1030 and related federal criminal laws*, Congressional Research Service, www.fas.org/sgp/crs/misc/RS20830.pdf. [Accessed 20/08/13]

Greenberg, A. (2013) Lily Collins Tops Most Harmful Celebrity Web Searches, *SC Magazine*, 19 September, www.scmagazineuk.com/lily-collins-tops-most-harmful-celebrity-web-searches/article/312313/?DCMP=EMC-SCUK_Newswire. [Accessed 19/09/13]

Hafner, K. and Markoff, J. (1995) *Cyberpunk – Outlaws and Hackers on the Computer Frontier*, New York, Simon & Schuster.

Information Commissioner's Office (2012) *Notification of Data Security Breaches to the Information Commissioner's Office (ICO)*, www.ico.org.uk/~/media/documents/library/Data_Protection/Practical_application/BREACH_REPORTING.ashx. [Accessed 28/08/13]

irchelp.org (2012) *Trojan Horse Attacks*, www.irchelp.org/irchelp/security/trojan.html. [Accessed 13/10/13]

Kerner, S. M. (2013) Kevin Mitnick Details Modern IT Threats, *Eweek*, 29 August, www.eweek.com/security/kevin-mitnick-details-modern-it-threats.html. [Accessed 02/09/13]

Levy, S. (1984) *Hackers: heroes of the computer revolution*, Garden City, NY, Anchor.

Mitnick, K. D. (2002) *The Art of Deception: controlling the human element of security*, Indianapolis, IN, Wiley.

Mitnick, K. D. (2005) *The Art of Intrusion: the real stories behind the exploits of hackers, intruders and deceivers*, Indianapolis, IN, Wiley.

Ponemon Institute (2013) *2013 Cost of Data Breach Study: global analysis*, www..symantec.com/about/news/resources/press_kits/detail.jsp?pkid=ponemon-2013. [Accessed 05/04/14]

Raymond, E. (2001) *How to Become a Hacker*, Thyrsus Enterprises, www.catb.org/esr/faqs/hacker-howto.html#what_is. [Accessed 04/10/13]

Raywood, D. (2013) An Inside Job: the danger that lurks within, *SC Magazine*, 23 August, www.scmagazineuk.com/an-inside-job-the-danger-that-lurks-within/article/308567/?DCMP=EMC-SCUK_Newswire. [Accessed 28/08/13]

Sawyer, J. (2013) How Attackers Target and Exploit Social Networking Users, *Information Week Reports*, August, http://reports.informationweek.com/abstract/21/11235/Security/How-Attackers-Target-and-Exploit-Social-Networking-Users.html. [Accessed 18/09/13]

Silowash, G., Cappelli, D., Moore, A., Trzeciak, R., Shimeall, T. and Flynn, L. (2012) *Common Sense Guide to Mitigating Insider Threats*, 4th edn, Technical Report CMU/SEI-2012-TR-012, Pittsburgh, PA, Software Engineering Institute, Carnegie Mellon University, www.sei.cmu.edu/library/abstracts/reports/12tr012.cfm. [Accessed 05/04/14]

Tait, J. (2013) Judge Sentences Bradley Manning to 35 years, *Washington Post*,

21 August, www.washingtonpost.com/world/national-security/judge-to-sentence-bradley-manning-today/2013/08/20/85bee184-09d0-11e3-b87c-476db8ac34cd_story.html. [Accessed 23/08/13]

Vaughan-Nichols, S. J. (2013) *Linux Desktop Trojan 'Hand of Thief' Steals in*, Linux and Open Source blog, ZDNet, www.zdnet.com/blog/open-source. [Accessed 09/07/13]

Weinberger, S. (2012) Top Ten Most Destructive Computer Viruses, *Smithsonian Magazine*, 20 March, www.smithsonianmag.com/science-nature/Top-Ten-Most-Destructive-Computer-Viruses.html. [Accessed 06/09/13]

Wood, S. (2011) *Acceptable Use Policy*, https://community.ja.net/library/acceptable-use-policy. [Accessed 17/10/13]

CHAPTER 5

Security, risk management and business continuity

Introduction

> In terms of its inherent nature, security is sometimes described as an emergent property of networks and the organizations they support. Given security's many dimensions, the precise location where security is enacted cannot be readily identified. An organization's security condition is often determined in the interaction and intersection of people, processes, and technology. As the organization and the underlying network infrastructure change in response to the evolving risk environment, so will the state of an entity's security.
>
> Allen and Westby, 2007, 15

This chapter goes hand in hand with Chapter 4, which described threats to our information, and how to deal with them. It would be understandable to take the view that, having addressed the issue of threats, our organization is now secure, and this type of reactive approach is widespread. However, as in so many other areas of business, the external environment is changing, and expectations are changing, too.

If we examine the idea of 'security' a bit more closely, taking an individual person as an analogy, security doesn't just mean locking the doors and windows of the house at night, and setting burglar alarms, though of course those are important elements. A person would like to be physically secure when outside the house, dealing with other people. He or she would like to be secure in their employment, to be treated fairly in business dealings, to be respected as a member of society. At whatever level of abstraction we examine the individual's interactions with their environment, there is an implicit notion of security as perceived freedom from concerns. This perceived freedom, though, will have been accomplished by the actions of many individuals, in their creation and maintenance of a society in which freedom is possible. Or, if you prefer, threats are like illnesses, which impact on our desired state of health. There is more to health than the avoidance and treatment of illnesses, although these are large factors in maintaining health.

Similarly, there isn't a security process, it's more a way of doing the business processes. You could say what we want is not security in the sense of bars on the windows, though that might be part of it, nor in the sense of border controls, though that might be part of it, nor in the sense of being able to yell, 'Security!' and have a specialized team rush to our assistance, though that might be part of it, too. We want security in the sense of feeling secure about our business, and the way we do business, and there are many factors which contribute to that.

The point is that security is a much bigger issue than installing a firewall and using good passwords. Security means being able to conduct your business as you see fit, within the constraints imposed by society for the general security of all. Anything which impinges upon your ability to function 'healthily' is a security issue. But this chapter is separate from the last one because security is concerned with much more than simply responding to threats: it involves a way of viewing an organization which is quite different both to traditional views and to other operational views.

The pay-off for security is assurance. Here is a description of what Information Assurance means to the US Department of Defense:

> 1.2. All DoD information systems shall maintain an appropriate level of confidentiality, integrity, authentication, non-repudiation, and availability that reflect a balance among the importance and sensitivity of the information and information assets; documented threats and vulnerabilities; the trustworthiness of users and interconnecting systems; the impact of impairment or destruction to the DoD information system; and cost effectiveness.
>
> US Department of Defense, 2007, 3

You may recognize there some of the characteristics of an authoritative record, from Chapter 2, and some of the requirements placed upon data processors by the relevant authorities, such as the Information Commissioner's Office. The quest for assurance is the driving force behind all our efforts towards good information governance, and the key elements behind assurance, all of which can be identified in that paragraph, are security, risk management and business continuity.

The security environment

Price Waterhouse Cooper's (2013) survey of UK information security breaches found that the number of breaches continues to increase, in almost all respects, with 93% of large businesses (those with more than 250 employees) and 87% of small businesses (those with fewer than 50 employees) reporting a security breach in the last year. While the numbers for large organizations are comparable over the two years, those for small businesses have risen from 76%. Tables 5.1 and 5.2 show the analysis of the types of attack which go to make up these percentages. Some threats will be counted under more than one category.

Table 5.1 2012/13 attacks on large businesses (adapted from Price Waterhouse Cooper, 2013)		
Large (>250 employees) businesses		
Attack	2012	2013
By an unauthorized outsider	73%	78%
Denial of service	30%	29%
Outsiders penetrated network	15%	20%
Outsiders have stolen IP or confidential data	12%	14%

Table 5.2 2012/13 attacks on small businesses (adapted from Price Waterhouse Cooper, 2013)		
Small (<50 employees) businesses		
Attack	2012	2013
By an unauthorized outsider	41%	63%
Denial of service	15%	23%
Outsiders penetrated network	7%	15%
Outsiders have stolen IP or confidential data	4%	9%

The cost to a large organization of its worst security breach for the year varied from £450,000 to £850,000; for small businesses, from £35,000 to £65,000.

The sources of attacks were internal as well as external, and PCW note that '[s]erious security breaches are often due to multiple failures in technology, processes and people' (see Table 5.3).

Table 5.3 2012/13 sources of security breaches in small businesses (adapted from Price Waterhouse Cooper, 2013)		
Small(<50 employees) businesses		
	2012	2013
Inadvertent human error	Not recorded	36%
Staff-related security breaches	45%	57%
Know their staff broke Data Protection regulations in the last year	11%	17%

To give these statistics a financial context, when investigating the impact on stock prices of 'cyber-attacks', the US Congressional Research Service discovered that in the days following an attack, identified target firms suffered losses of between 1 and 5%. This equates to between $50 million and $200 million for the average New York Stock Exchange corporation (Allen and Westby, 2007).

So, we can see from the tables that everyone is vulnerable, not only the 'big names' – being a small organization doesn't mean that you escape the attention of attackers. This is partly to do with how targets are identified – some attackers will deliberately target a big organization to prove a point, to gain prestige amongst their peers, or simply because big organizations have a lot of money to tempt them. However, many attacks will result from a program scanning through IP addresses (which uniquely identify computers attached to the internet) until they find one in use, and then searching for vulnerable applications running at that address. You don't have to advertise to attract attackers, and any machine with a fixed IP address is equally vulnerable.

The other implication is that the financial loss resulting from the loss of prestige from being identified as the target of a successful attack – unsuccessful attacks are not reported – is considerable, and therefore it is not surprising that organizations might be reluctant to report attacks. This, in turn, means that the statistics we see are probably an underestimate of the actual number of attacks taking place.

This, then, is why assurance is important in this context – if shareholders and other organizations who might consider doing business with us can see from our certification that we meet high standards of security, they are more likely to see us as a 'safe bet' to invest in or to trade with.

Strategy and tactics

One of the diagrams much beloved of the authors of management texts is a triangle showing the hierarchical structure of a typical organization (Figure 5.1). Nearer the base of the triangle, the greater width usually represents a large number of 'shop-floor' employees, and a large number of transactions. When describing information systems, this is the level where transaction processing systems (TPS) operate, recording sales, or library loans, or customer enquiries, depending on the context.

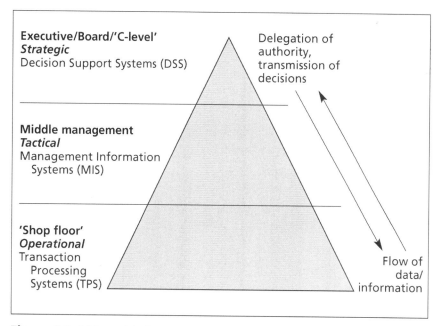

Figure 5.1 A hierarchical management structure, with information systems and flows

The middle area represents middle management, fewer in number, but more influential, and making decisions which are based partly on what goes on at the lower level, and partly on what is passed down from the level above. Their decisions are 'tactical' – they relate largely to the day-to-day running of the organization, and will be concerned with matters such as staffing, short-term budgeting and general operations. Their decision-making process may be aided by a management information system (MIS), which may use, as part of its input, the output of the TPS.

In the rarefied atmosphere at the top of the triangle, the executive managers operate. They are fewer in number than middle managers, and have more influence. They deliberate about strategic matters, looking at the long term, determining organizational policy, guiding the organization through its interactions with the external environment (legislation, economics, competition, etc.) and making high-level, or executive decisions. These decisions may be guided by a decision support system (DSS), which may use, as part of its input, the output of the MIS.

We see data gathered at the lower level being abstracted and summarized to information in the middle level, and ideally to knowledge and perhaps even wisdom at the top. The corresponding downward flow is a transmission of decisions and delegation of authority.

Of course, not only the executive level interacts with the outside world – the lower level carries out transactions with customers, the middle level organizes supplies from suppliers, and so on, but the executive level – 'the board', 'the management' – is the public face of the organization, and the 'brains' behind its operations. Neither, despite the 'executive' label, are these the only individuals who actually 'do things' – there is, typically, 'harder work' going on, the further we move down the triangle – but the things they do represent the organization as a whole.

The terms 'strategy' and 'tactics' derive from the military environment, where tactical decisions are concerned with operational matters, such as the conduct of a skirmish or a battle, whereas strategic decisions are concerned with a war or a campaign – larger and longer-term, and the province of generals, rather than more junior officers.

Security is a strategic matter

Changes in the environment in the last 20 years have brought about the situation where information security is now a strategic matter. It must be a concern of the board, the executive, the generals (quite literally, because there are military implications quite as pressing as any in business), and their influence must drive the establishment of a security culture throughout the organization.

Of course security is a concern at lower levels in the organization just as is interaction with the outside world. Indeed, security needs to lie behind all interaction with the outside world. Security must be behind all transactions with customers, it must be a factor in 'hiring and firing' and in dealing with suppliers, and at the same time, it must be the bedrock of the business, the foundation upon which all internal functions and external operations are based.

Security can no longer be seen as the responsibility of the IT department, any more than individuals should trust their lives to a locksmith. There is an aspect of security which relies on IT, but your locksmith is not expected to protect you from a riot in the street, or from the collapse of your pension fund, and your IT department is not responsible for the actions of your employees, much less those of your business partners' employees.

Good reputations are hard-earned – they have to be based on the experience of a large number of interactions. In today's business world, there is an imperative that results are achieved quickly, and even the time it takes to research a reputation is precious, let alone the time it takes to establish one. We have seen in earlier chapters some of the responsibilities that organizations have towards the data and information they handle, and we have seen that these responsibilities are sometimes transferable to other organizations. We have looked at the importance of the quality of an organization's data, and we can extend that to include data originating with other organizations or being transferred to them.

Security is not only a matter for our own organization; it also influences who we deal with, and how we deal with them. Given the threats to security we have considered in the last chapter, it is probably inevitable that breaches will occur – as we have just seen, they can be a result of actions which are no fault of our own. In the event of a security breach, the way that it is handled can be just as influential on an organization's reputation, and even its continued existence, as the fact that the breach occurred in the first place, so in this chapter we shall also look at business continuity – what to do when what may be the inevitable happens.

A body of opinion, dating from about the year 2004, proposed that information security is so vital that it should be a major concern at the executive level of organizations, and should be enshrined in a corporate information security governance framework, perhaps structured after the model provided by International Standards Organization's (ISO) ISO 17799 (Information Technology – Security Techniques – Code of Practice for Information Security Management). In other words, security should be seen not as a technological challenge, but as a corporate governance issue. ISO standards are expensive to purchase, but if you have access to a research or business library, they may have hard copies, or a subscription allowing users to download copies without charge. Alternatively, some countries publish online their version of the standards, which often differs from the ISO only in that it has the country's name in the title. This is an information retrieval exercise that can reduce your expenditure.

Case study – Entrust

Entrust (2004) is a case study that provides a good description of the implementation of an information security governance (ISG) system in a US organization which is itself a provider of security solutions worldwide. Entrust was fortunate in that it started from a position where F. W. Conner, who is both Chairman and Chief Executive Officer (CEO), was very supportive of, and indeed instigated, a review of its internal security practices. It was found that there was no internal ISG framework, and the organization set about creating one built upon best practices. They conducted 'an extensive literature review' of best practice in the USA and other countries, focusing on technical, security professional, audit and governance, government initiatives and other standards, such as the International Information Society's Generally

Accepted System Security Principles (GASSP), the National Institute of Standards and Technology (NIST) and ISO. They mapped people, process and technology aspects of their organization against operational, tactical and strategic objectives, eventually choosing ISO 17799 as the 'best reference' for ISG. However, they found that although ISO 17799 stated the importance of management involvement in information security, it, and indeed most of the literature on information security, failed to address adequately strategic people and process issues. Translating this out of management-speak, they found that ISO 17799 was helpful on operational and tactical issues (the lower two-thirds of the management triangle) regarding people, processes and technology, and also on strategic issues regarding technology, but weaker regarding non-technical, strategic issues. In even simpler terms, they identified a gap where the executive management should have been involved.

Entrust identified three 'cycles of continuous improvement', noting a parallel with quality improvement practices, which are iterative, rather than 'one-off'. Cycle one involved identifying responsibilities and accountability through a high-level survey mapped onto the 10 chapters of ISO 17799 (later expanded into the 13 content sections of ISO 27002, listed below on pages 125 and 126). The 'high-level' nature of the survey avoids a danger of it becoming mired in points of detail. Risks in each area (for example, security policy, personnel security, access control) were simply identified as red, yellow or green, denoting high, medium and low. This allowed the organization to focus on important areas, at a level of detail which was appropriate for consideration by the board of directors, and allowed senior managers to make key decisions without being 'told what to do' by the IT Group.

Cycle two identified key systems in each business area, and carried out a further risk survey, at the next level of detail from ISO 17799. This 'pass' looked at 'what people actually do rather than what the policies say'.

Cycle three consisted of short reviews with each business group (for example, sales, marketing, IS/IT), identifying the information systems and resources needed to accomplish the business group's mission and objectives relative to the company's mission and objectives.

So, overall, we can see that the process surveys the organization at increasing levels of detail, identifying roles and responsibilities at each level, and identifying areas and severities of risk, then establishing what has to be done in order to remediate those risks.

Lessons to be learned

Entrust (2004) is very informative regarding tips for implementing an ISG process, but it is reasonable to ask what relevance an organization-wide rethink, amounting to business process re-engineering, has to the information manager in a smaller organization.

F. W. Conner, the Chairman and CEO of Entrust, co-chaired a task force of software companies, and their report, the Business Software Alliance's (2003) paper *Information Security Governance: toward a framework for action* appears to have been highly influential. It made the point that, in the USA at least, the problem with security was not a lack of legislation which could be applied – there were already the Sarbanes-Oxley Act of 2002, covering the internal controls against security breaches and public disclosures of security breaches of public companies subject to US security laws, the Gramm-Leach-Bliley Act of 1999, covering the security of customer records in financial institutions, the California Database Security Breach Information Act (SB 1386), covering the reporting of breaches of personal information in that state, the Federal Information Security Management Act, covering federal information systems and security programs, and the (then pending) Health Insurance Privacy and Accountability Act. The paper observed that between them these acts covered financial, personal, health, customer and government information, and mandated civil and criminal penalties, as well as giving rights to private action. It also noted that ISO 17799 provided broad guidance on implementing information security, but had to be tailored to each company's needs according to their risk assessment.

Not every organization has a chief executive as aware of the centrality of security as Mr Conner, but the ISG process does not have to be instigated from the top – the important thing is that there is buy-in from the executive level. The Entrust case study shows that a system of cycles, which begin at a general level and then become more specific to individual departments, can present an appropriate amount of information to each level of management, so that responsibilities and accountabilities can be identified, and uncertainties addressed in order of urgency, without overloading any single level with detail. This kind of analysis and reporting is exactly where information management can fit into the process – it is, after all, a very similar exercise to the information audit and records audit which inform the records management process, and enable the organization to ensure compliance with legislation, as discussed in Chapter 2.

In ISO 17799, Entrust had a tool which was partially, but not completely, fit for purpose. We shall now discuss the current standards, and discover that this shortfall is being addressed.

Standards – the ISO 27000 series

As indicated in the preceding case study, ISO 17799 was mainly concerned with security controls. It had a corresponding British Standard, BS7799, which itself had an associated standard, BS7799-2, concerned more with security systems. This latter standard later, in 2005, evolved into ISO 27001.

The ISO 27000 series of standards has been developed jointly by the International Organization for Standardization (ISO) and the International Electrotechnical Commission (IEC) to deal with information security matters. The publications are therefore properly known as 'ISO/IEC 27000: 2012', and so on (the final group of numbers signifying the date of publication), but the commonly used and somewhat less cumbersome form 'ISO 27000' will be used here. It is intended to fit in with other 'families' of standards, such as ISO 9000, which is concerned with quality management, and ISO 14000, concerned with environmental management. Here, we can see the new 'positioning' of security – it is increasingly likely to be a requirement that an organization must meet certain standards of security before other organizations will do business with it, in the same way that many organizations require that their business partners meet ISO 9001 for quality management, or ISO 14001 for environmental management.

Because the standards are international, and are independently assessed, they translate across international boundaries, and provide the same level of assurance everywhere, independent of local variations in legislation, for example. The second edition, ISO 27000: 2012, which gives an overview and defines a vocabulary for the series, is freely available as an electronic copy from the ISO/IEC (2012).

It is clear from ISO 27000: 2012 that the breadth of coverage of the series exceeds what might be expected. For example, an 'asset' – 'anything that has value to the organization' can include 'services . . . people and their qualifications, skills, and experience; and . . . intangibles, such as reputation and image' (ISO/IEC, 2012, 2). Assets require protection 'against the loss of availability, confidentiality and integrity. Enabling accurate and complete information to be available in a timely manner to those with an authorized need is a catalyst for business efficiency' (ISO/IEC, 2012, 11). In other words, security of information is concerned with protecting it not only from theft, but also from anything which might compromise its availability, confidentiality and integrity. Our business is more efficient when complete and accurate information is available to the right people, at the right time. If this is not the case, there is a security problem.

When we take this viewpoint, the question of information security opens up dramatically. Information is not just what is encoded in data files or in hard copy – it might be tacit knowledge possessed by an employee. It can be transmitted electronically, but also by courier, or word of mouth.

The series continues with ISO 27001, which specifies an information security management system (ISMS), and provides 'a model for establishing, implementing, operating, monitoring, reviewing, maintaining, and improving an Information Security Management System'. Systems may be certified against this standard, and more than a thousand have been since its introduction in October 2005, as a replacement for the old British Standard BS7799-2. Some certification agencies provide for conversion from certification under the old standard to certification under the new one.

ISO 27001: 2005 has a 'process approach', which deals with applying processes across an organization, and identifying the processes and how they interact and are managed. It uses the plan-do-check-action model, a variant on the 'life-cycle' models familiar from other contexts such as software development. So ISO 27001 is involved with evaluation, planning, and implementing processes. The new edition, ISO 27001: 2013, has a greater emphasis on measuring and evaluating the performance of an ISMS. Material on outsourcing has been added, and there is more emphasis on the organizational context of the systems. The content sections are:

- Context of the organization
- Information security leadership
- Planning an ISMS
- Support
- Operation
- Performance evaluation
- Improvement
- Annex A – List of controls and their objectives.

As can be seen from the contents, particularly in the light of the definitions from ISO 27000, the scope of the ISMS is organizational, and the decision to adopt an ISMS is a strategic one. We can see from the next standard that the impact of the system is organization-wide, and only support and commitment at boardroom level can ensure its successful adoption.

ISO 27002 is concerned with the controls and mechanisms by which these processes may be implemented – it is intended to be complementary to ISO 27001. The content sections are:

- Structure
- Risk assessment and treatment
- Security policy
- Organization of information security
- Asset management
- Human resources security
- Physical security
- Communications and operations management
- Access control

- Information systems acquisition, development, maintenance
- Information security incident management
- Business continuity
- Compliance.

Some of these may seem more obviously concerned with information than others, but all are concerned with information systems.

The series of standards continues with:

- ISO 27003 – guidance as to the implementation of an ISMS: establishing, implementing, reviewing and improving it. Again, we see that the cyclical nature of the process is made explicit in the structure of the standard itself. Systems are never simply designed, implemented, and left in place – there is always a review-and-improve stage, which feeds back to the beginning of the cycle. This reviewing is aided by ISO 27004, which looks at developing metrics and carrying out measurements to gauge the effectiveness of the system.
- ISO 27005 provides guidelines for information security risk management, but does not put forward a specific methodology, being intended for use by all types of organization.
- ISO 27006 sets out the requirements for bodies which carry out registration and certification of organizations with respect to their ISMS, whilst ISO 27007 sets out the guidelines for carrying out the auditing.

Other standards have been published regarding guidelines on implementation for various parties involved in the certification process, and on implementation in various industry sectors (such as health services), and it is intended that further standards will be added to this series. Many more are currently in preparation.

Practical measures

Full-blown ISO certification may not be within the reach of every organization – it may be too costly, or too onerous, or the required buy-in at executive management level may simply be lacking. However, this does not mean that security is a lost cause at operational and tactical levels. Let's think about a cut-down model, and start with identifying roles and responsibilities. If we take a department-by-department look at the organization, and identify the information each department handles, we can then ask what is being done by each department to fulfil its responsibilities regarding that information. Indeed, we might start by examining each department's awareness of those responsibilities.

A different, and complementary, approach is to 'follow the data' – look at the flow of information through the organization, for example a student's data from initial enquiry through to archiving of results transcript, and track the procedures which are applied at each stage to ensure security. This might be termed a 'horizontal slice' through the organization, as opposed to the previous, 'vertical', department-oriented approach. This should be done in a spirit of working towards higher standards, not of recrimination for substandard practices. After all, there are frequent changes to legislation, and there are probably frequent changes to staffing, which themselves are sufficient to justify a rolling program of education and re-evaluation of practices.

Having identified where there may be uncertainty as to who is responsible for particular aspects of security, most of what needs to be done is educational and procedural, rather than the application of any technological wizardry. However, there are physical and technological aspects which must be attended to.

Physical security

As discussed in the previous chapter, physical security of computer equipment and the media on which data is transferred is essential to system security. If someone can gain physical access to a computer, you may as well assume that they can get access to any data stored on the computer, and, in many cases, on networks to which the computer is connected. Strong encryption can delay re-use of the data, but should not be relied upon. It should, however, be a requirement, and a matter of policy, that sensitive data removed from a secure workplace should be encrypted. Encryption of hard copies probably only happens in wartime and in spy stories, but that does not excuse a lack of care. The bulk of hard copies compared to computer media tends to remind people not to leave them lying around, but it has always happened, and no doubt always will. It is also worth noting that a popular tactic with crackers of the Mitnick era (see Chapter 4) was, and no doubt continues to be, 'dumpster diving' – searching through industrial and office waste for discarded manuals and printouts. Shredding as a part of the disposal of printed sensitive material ought to be a matter of policy. There has been a shift in recent times towards more people working at home, and it is important to recognize that material taken home to work on is subject to the same security issues as if it were in the office. If it is not to be kept securely, it ought not to be leaving the premises.

Laptop computers, smartphones and tablets are a relatively recent potential weakness in the organizational armour. These are frequently used to access wireless networks, and perhaps e-mail accounts, at work, as well as at home, and are often, if not usually, set up with appropriate login details to do so. If these devices are stolen or lost, and they are not password protected, that is potentially a major breach of security. Even if they are password protected, we have seen in Chapter 4, section 5.4, that this is, at best, a delaying measure, and provision should be made for the reporting of such events and the immediate 'locking down' of affected accounts.

Back-ups

The practice of taking data back-ups is the core of information security. Even if a machine is stolen or destroyed, properly backed-up data can be used to restore operations to normal, once replacement hardware is available. The anecdotal evidence is that people are very undisciplined about backing-up data on their personal machines, and usually begin the practice only when they suffer serious inconvenience as a result of not backing-up. They then perform back-ups with great diligence, which tails off in time until the next data loss, after which the cycle is repeated.

More important machines, such as servers, will probably use technologies such as disk striping and RAID (redundant array of independent disks), which are hardware measures to guard against data loss; or 'customer-facing' services, in particular, may employ 'failover' – duplicate equipment with duplication of data, which can be immediately employed in the event of failure in the operational equipment. These are technically more robust than older systems, but they are still isolated systems, and still vulnerable to site-wide disasters.

There is no good reason to assume that people will be any more careful with data belonging to their employer – rather the reverse, because they have no real personal investment in its integrity. It might be annoying to have to repeat work, but they are still paid to do so.

Quite simply, this mindset, whilst perfectly understandable, must not be allowed to dictate practices regarding back-ups in the workplace. There are well established and effective practices which can and should be adopted, and which will preserve business continuity as regards data in the event of all but the most complex series of misfortunes, or the most determined malicious actions.

Full back-up

A full back-up is self-explanatory – all data on the system is copied to a removable medium, often tape. It is good practice to store a copy of this back-up in a secure, off-site location, in case of physical disaster (for example, fire or flood) affecting the main site.

A full back-up will probably be time-consuming, and it is unlikely to be necessary to perform one very frequently, because a large proportion of the data in a typical system does not change on a day-to-day basis.

A full back-up of the complete system (applications and data) might be taken as a means of restoring a system to a known working configuration, or as a means of installing a standard 'build' onto new machines on a network, but this is usually termed 'system imaging'.

Several full back-ups will be preserved, so that system states from earlier times may be recovered – this might be necessary in the event of a legal requirement to produce historical records, and so the back-up policy must be integrated with records retention schedules, which were discussed in Chapter 2.

Incremental back-up

An incremental back-up is taken more frequently – as the name implies, incremental back-ups are cumulative, and preserve changes made since the last full or incremental back-up. Restoring the system involves restoring the last full back-up, then restoring, in turn, all incremental back-ups taken since the last full back-up.

For example, a Library Management System (LMS) might be fully backed up every month, and an incremental back-up taken every night (back-ups are often scheduled at times when systems are typically used less, because the back-up might impact upon system performance), recording the day's transactions (issues and returns). In the event of system failure, the last full back-up is restored, followed by each day's incremental back-up, in sequence, until the time of the system failure.

Because of the frequent nature of incremental back-ups and the need to restore all taken since the last full back-up, an alternative practice is to use differential back-ups.

Differential back-up

A differential back-up saves all data changes since the last full back-up. This has the advantage that, at most, two restorations of data have to be made – the latest full back-up, plus the latest differential back-up. The downside is that the longer it has been since the last full back-up, the longer it will take to make, and ultimately to restore, the differential back-up.

Back-up media

As stated earlier, tape is a popular back-up medium, now more often encountered in cassette or cartridge form than in the older-style reels. It is important to remember that tape back-up is only possible where tape drives are installed, which usually means on servers, which in turn means that network drives are backed up, rather than the hard drives on individual computers. For this reason, it is important that network drives are used for storing organizational data. When there are reasons why access should be limited to particular users, this can be arranged by allocating access permissions, which is a system administrator's responsibility. If data must be stored on individual hard drives, perhaps when employees are working at home or without network connectivity to the organization, or in contexts such as a mobile library, or a branch of an organization which has lost its network connection to the main branch, CDs, DVDs and USB devices are potential back-up media, but good back-up discipline must be observed, and attention paid to the encryption of sensitive data, as necessary.

As mentioned earlier, at least one copy of back-up media should be stored off-site, as far as possible in appropriately secure and fire-, water- and generally disaster-proof premises. The off-site premises should not be an employee's home, nor should the same employee be responsible for back-up and restoration of data, thus reducing risk from malicious, or incompetent, actions by employees. Whatever media are employed, back-ups and restoration must be tested.

Cloud back-up

Taking 'off-site' to the extreme, cloud computing now offers the possibility of storage and back-up 'in the cloud' – that is, hosted remotely on dedicated equipment owned and operated by third parties. There are arguments for and against this option. On the plus side, it can be an extremely convenient solution, the actual operation can be handled by dedicated staff, working to service-level agreements and dedicated data centres are likely to be equipped with better physical and electronic security than most individual organizations can provide. You can choose a supplier that is ISO 27001-certified, which provides some assurance of reliability. For an extensive discussion of security measures taken by a large-scale, cloud-based library operation, see OCLC (n. d.). On the negative side, there is cost, and the data must travel across networks, which may vary in security, as regards unauthorized access. The data are stored at an unspecified location, or locations, 'in the cloud', so that they may be subject to the laws of a different jurisdiction – for example, it has happened that organizations using a cloud service have been unable to access their data because it shares storage with the data of another organization under official investigation, and the server has effectively been impounded. There is also a risk of a fellow 'occupant' of the storage being able to access your data. We have seen in Chapter 2 that when dealing with sensitive personal data, EU organizations are effectively prohibited from exporting them to legislatures which do not adhere to standards comparable with those in the EU. When data are in the cloud, the exact whereabouts of their storage may be difficult to determine, as may the matter of what laws apply to them. Also, the cloud provider itself may, despite its security, be subject to a disaster – perhaps data in the cloud should also be backed up elsewhere, in which case, is it a feasible solution? In any case, as with local back-up, cloud back-up and restoration must be tested regularly.

As cloud computing increases in popularity, issues such as these are likely to arise with increasing frequency. Until best practice in this area is established, it may be wise to be cautious about reliance on cloud solutions.

Security analysis is particularly important when hosting data and operations in the cloud. Do you actually know what data are there, what operations are being performed there, and what ports on your firewall are open? Cloud services are not transparent about their security provision, and may not give easy log access. They may, however, have the newest and best security equipment, and use that as a selling point. They need to have security right, so there is a big incentive for them. They don't have the legacy kit and they're starting from scratch and designing what they do at the same time as the security, rather than bolting security on to IT. You should also consider contracts – who owns the data, and how do you get them out again? What are their, and your, disaster recovery plans? At the moment, you can outsource responsibility, not accountability. After 2015, the same level of obligation will pass to the cloud service providers, and they will have to prove compliance. The better ones will be open about allowing testing and sharing what they do. The US government's PRISM program, and the Patriot Act, may deter EU businesses from US-hosted cloud solutions, because they threaten to require that the government be given access to data stored on US servers.

A final thought on back-ups

In the rest of this chapter, we shall be considering risk management and business continuity management, and back-ups are central to both of these processes. They have been dealt with separately partly for that reason, but principally because they are such a central element of information security that they should be considered as part of normal operations, not as a remedy for errors. By the time that requirement arises, unless there is a back-up policy in place, it is too late.

Risk management

The risk management process enables the organization to identify risks and to take appropriate steps to act on them, if necessary, ideally with a view to managing them in such a way that nobody even realizes that a risk has occurred. The relevant standard in this case is ISO 31000, *Risk Management Principles and Guidelines* (ISO/IEC, 2009a), which follows the familiar pattern of assessment, design and implementation, review and modification, or plan-do-check-act (Figure 5.2).

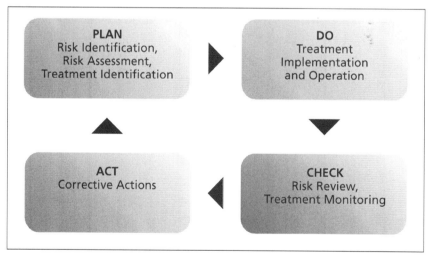

Figure 5.2 The plan-do-check-act cycle (Northwest Controlling Corporation Ltd, 2012)

According to ISO 31000:

Evaluating the organization's internal context may include, but is not limited to:

- governance, organizational structure, roles and accountabilities;
- policies, objectives, and the strategies that are in place to achieve them;
- capabilities, understood in terms of resources and knowledge (e.g. capital, time, people, processes, systems and technologies);
- information systems, information flows and decision making processes (both formal and informal)
- relationships with, and perceptions and values of, internal stakeholders;
- the organization's culture;
- standards, guidelines and models adopted by the organization; and
- the form and extent of contractual relationships.

(ISO/IEC, 2009a)

So note that information systems are part of the internal context of the organization in which we may want to design and implement a risk management framework. They can influence the design of the framework, according to the standard. The standard is written at quite a high, almost idealistic level, in keeping with its declared aim to be of service to all types of organization.

It is important to understand when discussing risk management that risks are not the same as threats. A risk as defined by the Institute of Risk Management (IRM) is the combination of the probability of an event and the consequences of the event, so the consequences are not necessarily negative, although we will tend to be concerned more about those which are. ISO 31000 says that a risk is 'the effect of uncertainty on objectives' (ISO/IEC, 2009a), this effect being positive, negative or a deviation from the expected. Different disciplines define risks differently, and also subdivide them differently.

Types of risk

The subdivision used in ISO Guide 73 (ISO/IEC 2009b), which is a list of definitions pertaining to the standard, divides risks into hazard risks, control risks and opportunity risks.

Hazard risks

Hazard risks, as the name suggests, may result in negative outcomes. They may also be thought of as 'operational risks', and are the kinds of event which are sufficiently recognized as being risks in the organization's operations that it is often the case that they can be insured against. For example, a library might have a (grudging) expectation of losing a certain amount of material to theft. There will be a certain level of tolerance of this risk, which will be managed within the organization, and there may be an insurance policy which can be activated if this level of tolerance is exceeded – for example by the theft of one of the more prized items in the collection. A credit card company will be resigned to a certain level of risk that its cards will be used for fraudulent purchases, and will have to reimburse the parties defrauded, an expense which it may hedge off to insurers, or cover by raising interest rates.

Control risks

Control risks, or operational risks, or 'uncertainty risks', are concerned with uncertainty about outcomes, perhaps those resulting from project management or from a sales strategy. For example, an organization might decide to cut prices on some lines of items, in an attempt to boost sales of related lines. These risks can be managed, so that their outcomes fall within acceptable boundaries. Events might hinder the completion of a project, for example a contractor might pull out, or market circumstances might unexpectedly change.

Opportunity risks

Opportunity risks, or strategic risks, are different, in that they are undertaken voluntarily – risks on investments or on new business ventures, taken in the hope that the outcomes will be positive, rather than negative (Hopkin, 2012).

Handling risk

On examination of the ISO 31000 standard, we follow a familiar pattern, beginning with establishing a mandate and commitment, followed by:

- design of framework for managing risk (4.3)
- understanding the organization and its context (4.3.1)
- establishing risk management policy (4.3.2)
- accountability (4.3.3)
- integration into organizational processes (4.3.4)
- resources (4.3.5)
- establishing internal communication and reporting mechanisms (4.3.6)
- establishing external communication and reporting mechanisms (4.3.7).

and then implementation, monitoring and review and continual improvement – the life-cycle. The numbers in brackets are references to sections of the ISO 31000 standard.

According to Hopkin (2012, 49), risk management should be:

- Proportionate to the level of risk within the organization
- Aligned with other business activities
- Comprehensive, systematic and structured
- Embedded within business processes
- Dynamic, iterative and responsive to change.

These principles are summarized in the acronym PACED, and the deliverables in the acronym CADE3:

- Compliance with laws and regulations
- Assurance regarding the management of significant risks
- Decisions that pay full regard to risk considerations
- Efficiency, Effectiveness and Efficacy in operations, projects and strategy.

Hazard management, risk control and loss management are the ways to reduce the negativity of the outcome of hazard events, which are the type most likely to concern the information worker, and in the next section we consider some of the practical steps which can be taken towards these ends. Control management, reducing the range of outcomes from events, is accomplished by internal financial controls. Opportunity management is a strategic matter, and Hopkin (2012, 55) makes the point that, following the global financial crisis, undue risk-taking should not be excessively rewarded.

Implementation

ISO 31000 is informative about establishing a framework, but is quite general and high-level as regards implementation. It is not possible for an organization to be certified against the standard. There is also a British Standard, BS 31100, which provides advice on putting the principles described in ISO 31000 into practice. Although it offers advice on developing, implementing and maintaining a risk management system, Hopkin (2012, 52) says that it could be argued that while the two standards advise on 'the systematic application of management policies, procedures and practices to the tasks of communicating, consulting, establishing the context, identifying, analysing, evaluating, treating, monitoring and reviewing risk', the setting of policies, communication, etc., are more part of the framework than the process.

The establishment of a risk management framework and process is, as we have identified, another organization-wide undertaking, but in the immediate term, as regards process, Hopkins identifies four types of controls which provide a useful classification of things we can actually do to respond to hazard risks of the type occurring in an information context.

These control categories are Preventive, Corrective, Directive and Detective, and we can consider examples of each, with a view to incorporating them within our policy toolkit.

Preventive controls attempt to remove the source of a hazard, or to replace it with a less risky alternative. For example, a preventive control response to data breaches caused by staff human error might be to introduce pre-employment screening of staff.

Corrective control is achieved by moderating the circumstances leading to risks, for example limiting access to sensitive or valuable data by the use of passwords and access policies.

Directive controls, like corrective ones, are aimed at loss limitation and containment. For example, we might introduce advice on choice of 'good' passwords, or institute a 'bring your own device' (BYOD) policy to encourage responsible use of mobile devices, as we discussed in the last chapter (see also page 150). We also need to bear in mind that not all the important documents are electronic – there are things like charters, certificates, qualifications, which may be both irreplaceable and paper-based. If paper-based documentation is of significant value, we should also be thinking about things like fire sprinkler systems, inert gas fire response measures, and how documents can be protected as much as possible from water damage resulting from firefighting procedures. These may be eventualities that we find uncomfortable to contemplate, but being in the position of having thought them through is vastly preferable to having to deal with them on an ad hoc basis, whilst under the kind of pressure that a disaster inevitably brings.

Detective controls come into effect after the occurrence of a hazard, and are aimed at preventing its recurrence. They are not at an appropriate level to be considered as part of business continuity planning (BCP) or disaster recovery planning (DRP), but are suitable for responding to lower-level threats – for example stock checking can reveal dishonesty, internet log checking can expose unauthorized activity, and either can reveal risks while damage is still at an early stage. In fact, general awareness of the existence of such measures can act as a deterrent, so that they may also act as preventive controls.

Information and risk

As stated above, the risks which directly affect information workers are likely to be hazard risks, because information is a valuable commodity and there are many factors which are potential threats. We want to be in a position to deal with hazard-type threats; and here, we know, or we ought to know, what the risks are, at least in broad terms, because we have done the assessment and evaluation. Of course, there may still be surprises, but we should at least have identified the areas of threat from which these specific surprises come – crackers, denial of service, a compromised login – and know what steps to take.

However, it is also important to consider information, and information work, as a factor in managing the other types of risk. When we consider control risk or operational risk, the information manager can be the conduit, the mediator, the interpreter of information about the operational environment. The operational environment also plays a large part in the assessment of speculative risks. The information management function can be an asset to the organization's strategic program, part of the toolkit at their disposal. Information management can be the ear to the ground, the finger on the pulse, the early-warning system. This is part of risk assessment and risk identification, from the 'plan' part of the plan-do-check-act cycle, as well as part of review and monitoring, from the 'check' part. It is only through information that we can assess risk, and continue to evaluate changing risks.

Current awareness

Perhaps there is an opening to set up a current awareness program, tailored to organizational interests and functioning in a way analogous to the text messages some banks will send when your account is about to become overdrawn. Information management can do a lot in the area of operational and speculative risks, by becoming the organization's eyes and ears. The board's awareness of the business environment should not be solely through the board members' reading of *Time* or *Newsweek* or the *Financial Times* or *Forbes Magazine*, or through their social contacts, or even through their business contacts. Business intelligence is a legitimate area for the information professional, who has the retrieval and interpretative skills to find the most reliable and timely sources. We all know about the vast amounts of information 'out there', but finding it and making sense of it is a skilled job, and one at which information professionals can excel. The executives may read the right journals, but do they know which blogs have their finger on the pulse in your particular industry, or which LinkedIn groups are the most influential, or whom to follow on Twitter?

Let's look at a specific industry. If we consider the oil and gas industry, where 'operational risk' has a very literal meaning, there is a whole branch of supply chain management which concerns itself with prediction of operational failures in equipment, by using monitoring and statistical analysis. It has the same decisions to take about risks – if a piece of equipment might be about to fail, should it be overhauled, or replaced, with the associated 'downtime' for the operation, or does the operator accept the risk, and wait until the next opportunity to do maintenance during another scheduled period of downtime? Good decisions of this type are more frequently made by more experienced staff, suggesting that the statistics are not a panacea, but it is very hard to document the critical factors on which the decisions are based – these are very much 'unstructured data', which need to be interpreted. At a strategic level, in other industries, the same kinds of decisions might be made about withdrawing a service, or introducing a product line, but the sensors and monitors are not hardware – they are information tools.

The management of speculative risk involves the same sort of assessment, but projected into the future, and with a larger number of unknowns. If the board has strategic objectives such as developing a new market, then they will want to know if competitors are getting into the same area, or if not, why not (there may be a very good reason, that the board has not yet identified, why the market is not developed). They will want to know about any news which affects the projected areas of interest.

This is another aspect of governance – using information to our best advantage, making sure that the right information gets to the right people, at the right time. We don't want to flood the executives with every detail – executive summaries are so called for that reason – but we certainly want them to know about the important stuff. It is also assurance – the decision-makers can be assured that the decisions they make are based on the best, the most accurate, the most up-to-date information.

Information won't eliminate risk – without risk, there would be few benefits, because someone else would have claimed them. It can, though, reduce the perceived risk to the point where we feel able to take it on, because we are better informed than our competitors. Being 'better informed' is not a natural state, it's not a condition you're born into, but it is related to having a good source of information and using it properly.

Business continuity management (BCM)

In the event of severe incidents occurring, despite our best efforts to avert them, the next logical step in the process is business continuity management – the procedures which can be put in place to minimize disruption, whilst allowing the business to survive and continue.

There is a two-part British Standard, BS 25999 (British Standards Institute, 2006; 2007), which deals with BCM. The first part deals with understanding the processes, principles and terminology, the second with developing a strategy and developing and maintaining a plan. The second part was superseded in 2012 by the international standard ISO 22301. ISO 22301 is a standard against which organizations can be certified, in a two-part process. First, the documentation of the business continuity management system is reviewed, then the implementation of the plan is checked against the documentation.

Planning for BCM

Conforming to the standard means that businesses must plan, establish, implement, operate, monitor, review, maintain and continually improve a documented business continuity management system which allows them to plan for, respond to and recover from events that disrupt operations, as and when those events occur. There is an emphasis on the planning stage, and on the commitment required from management. The idea is that an organization develops a business continuity management system (BCMS) that conforms to its stated business continuity policy, and that it can demonstrate this conformity to others, either getting certification from an accredited third party certification body or making a self-declaration of conformity with the standard.

So, there is a requirement to look at the BCMS in relation to the internal and external factors that might affect its operation. This is not simply a matter of designing a plan and stating that you have a plan – it is not just a 'box-ticking' exercise. The organization is required to take into account its activities, business partners, supply chain and the impact of disruptive incidents. It must look at the relationship between the business continuity plan and other relevant policies, including its risk management strategy and its appetite for risk. The leadership of the business must demonstrate their commitment to the BCMS, including the provision of sufficient resources to establish, review and maintain it, and to communicate its importance throughout the business.

Developing a strategy

Having planned the BCMS, the organization can put it into operation, by carrying out a business impact analysis, which identifies the business's critical processes and their interdependencies, as well as the resources required to operate them at the minimum acceptable level. There will be a risk assessment, for which the ISO 31000 *Risk Management Principles and Guidelines* standard (discussed under 'Risk management', page 133) may be used. This step identifies, analyses and evaluates the risks of disruptive incidents.

Once these requirements are satisfied, a strategy can be developed which allows the business to protect and recover its critical activities within an acceptable time scale. The strategy should be aligned with the business's overall strategy, and it has been found that this is more likely to be the case the earlier that the BCM strategy is put in place.

Documenting procedures

The next step is to document the procedures involved in making sure that business activities can continue and disruption can be minimized in the event of a disruptive incident occurring. This includes communications inside and outwith the organization – who needs to be contacted, what they need to be told, what they need to be asked. Planning will take into account the availability of key personnel and how to contact them, the availability of alternative premises and replacement equipment, recovery of those vital off-site back-ups, the whereabouts of critical documents such as charters, leases and banking and tax information. There should be a plan of who needs to be contacted – emergency services, early on in the process, legal and financial representatives later.

Procedures include specific immediate actions to be taken, with enough flexibility to respond to unanticipated events and changing conditions, and should be developed based on the earlier survey of process interdependencies. They should serve to minimize disruption, by mitigating the consequences of the disruptive event (Professional Evaluation and Certification Board, 2012).

Testing

Like back-ups, this plan needs to be tested, and continually revised and maintained – in addition to the critical documents, it may be the most important document in your organization.

Planning for business continuity doesn't only have to mean continuity in the face of disaster, though – planning for continuity means that, as an organization, you plan still to be around in the long term. If disasters happen, they happen, but your organization is going to continue. Disaster management (DM) is a part of BCM, but not the only one. What you do for DM depends on the business, but essentially, you'll need to ensure (it's assurance, again) that you have access to the right people, to a place for them to work, to equipment for them to work with and to lines of communication for them to work through.

You need a 'shop front', real or virtual, so that customers and business partners see the continuity, or don't notice the discontinuity. Does your organization have enough confidence in its disaster management plan that it would do a 'live' test, just to check if anyone notices? If not, perhaps the plan is not sufficiently robust. Can you put a plan in place for your information service, such that the service can be maintained in the event of, for example, loss of service from an online database supplier, or even loss of internet connectivity? Maybe having a GPS-enabled tablet would be a useful back-up system, or you might want to investigate a reciprocal arrangement with neighbouring organizations to temporarily share each other's service in the event of an outage.

We want to be able to provide assurance to the rest of the organization, and for the organization to provide assurance to the world, that we can keep the business in continuous operation. This is something that is becoming more common, and hence, of course, is more commonly demanded, through well thought-out use of virtualization and cloud computing. Where there is a 'bricks and mortar' operation, the physical infrastructure needs to be catered for, but networking means that the information side of the business can be kept going, so that at least the online presence and the channels of communication are kept open. It's a service level that comes at a cost, if we are considering a 'failover' to a live image of our service 'in the cloud', but the costs must be weighed against potential loss of business, and the potentially much more costly damage to reputation, which could otherwise result.

Case study – Lettergold Plastics

Business continuity planning can also be helpful to businesses in aspects other than the possibility of a natural disaster, and it is important to recognize that what might appear to be far less dramatic incidents can have just as devastating an effect – in fact, this is part of the business impact analysis. Lettergold Plastics is a small UK engineering company, employing around 25 staff, and in 2008 it decided to adopt BS 25999 and has now transitioned to ISO 22301. This is in addition to its existing certification for ISO 9001, the quality management standard, ISO 14001 the environmental standard, and the health and safety standard OHSAS 1800. Its motivation to achieve certification was that a prospective customer stated this as a requirement for a tender, and the managing director said that the same requirement has arisen several times since then. He also said that before certification, any recovery plans existed only in his head, and that small businesses especially were often too reliant on individuals in this way. Lettergold's planning focused on the availability of its utilities, such as water, and the integrity of its supply chain, running an exercise which simulated the cessation of supply of crucial industrial chemicals, normally imported from Belgium. They identified a US source which could be used for the chemicals, although with associated, but acceptable, increases in costs and shipping time. The managing director believes that the test was very worthwhile and that the new BCM system is a great reassurance to the company itself, and to its customers. Now, whenever something new is introduced to their processes, they consider the implications for business continuity, so that they are better prepared for unexpected disruptions (BSI, 2013).

Business continuity in summary

We could say that business continuity is where the measures and standards we have been discussing really hit home – if the business cannot continue to operate successfully, nothing else matters. Putting BCM planning into place obviously involves a great deal of work and commitment – so much so that commitment is explicitly written into the ISO standard – but it should be regarded as a vital part of the organization's overall strategic planning. As seen in the case study above, it can provide assurance to those both within and outside the organization.

Policy

It appears that, when considering security, we have identified a number of standards which ought to be entrenched in the organization, and which can potentially be very effective when the will to employ them is present at the top, strategic levels of management. Whilst we must recognize that this level of buy-in may not always be present, it falls within the remit of an information management role to encourage adoption of best practices, and to educate colleagues in how best to follow them. There are, however, steps which can be taken, and policies formulated, which fall clearly under the aegis of information governance, and we make a start on setting those out here.

Back-ups

First of all, back-ups, as described under 'Back-ups' (see page 128), are essential to any security policy. It is preferable that work is saved to network drives, which can be more easily, or even automatically, backed up. As a minimum, a frequent full back-up must be stored securely off-site. Back-up and restore must be tested frequently, to ensure that both the integrity and the procedures are reliable. Multiple copies of back-ups should be kept, following one of the well established procedures. Restoring from a single, corrupt, back-up onto a live system is an effective way of destroying data, and the fact that the operator is unlikely to repeat the mistake is a small consolation.

Patches and updates

Because of improvements to their operating systems, or in order to release 'bug-fixes', or, increasingly, in order to address security issues, the suppliers of operating systems release software 'patches' to their systems. Microsoft usually do this on a Tuesday, hence 'Patch Tuesday', and updates to the Linux kernel (the core of the GNU/Linux operating system, which handles input/output requests and manages system devices) are released roughly every three months, though individual Linux suppliers may have their own release schedules.

These updates can often be applied automatically, for example by Microsoft Update or Linux System Update, although many IT departments prefer to evaluate the effects of new configurations themselves, or wait for peer reactions and feedback, before committing updates to their systems. The same processes are true of software applications packages – updates or 'bug fixes' are released, and may be offered as a download whilst the system is running. Indeed, this is more often the case than not.

Whilst caution in running the latest releases, which are untested in the public arena, may be laudable, it is still important that the administrators are aware of the releases, and of why they have been released, because it may be that they are intended to fix security 'holes' which will need attention in any case.

In October 2013, the software company Oracle, which supports the Java programming language and supplies many of the best-known database, middleware and virtualization products, announced in its three-monthly Critical Patch Update releases of 51 security updates to the Java language, and 76 updates to its other product families. Oracle is a huge organization, which supports a very large range of software, and this is reflected in the number of patches, but:

Fifty of those fixes [to Java] address vulnerabilities that can be exploited remotely without authentication and 12 of them have the highest possible severity rating which means they can be used to take complete control of the underlying operating system. . . . Two vulnerabilities were addressed in the Oracle Database Server and both can be exploited remotely without authentication and can result in partial compromise of data confidentiality.

Constantin (2013)

Oracle is not singled out here – it is just more visible because the scale of its operations means that its products are seen as more rewarding targets, because they are more commonly used. This is, of course, addressed by their Critical Patch Update releases, demonstrating a responsible attitude towards their customers, but the important point to note is that if the products of a large and reputable company, which has extensive resources to devote to product security, can be exploited to such an extent, then none of us can be relaxed about the threats to our systems, whoever the supplier. In this case, a temporary 'fix' was available – simply 'turning off' the permission to run Java programs from the browser addressed some of the issues. Maintaining awareness of current events in the world of security, therefore, and responding appropriately, is very important.

Energy Management Associates (2012) note that a large organization might have hundreds of thousands of 'endpoints' where there is an interface between humans and equipment. Put in a simpler way, the organization's network, which may extend worldwide, may have many and diverse pieces of equipment (PCs, terminals, tablets, smartphones, etc.) which are the places where the outside world interacts with the network (people operate the equipment). These endpoints are also potential entry points for malware and other threats, and it is important that the organization's security system is able to deliver and install patches, software updates and signature updates for anti-virus software ('signature' is the code identifying a virus), and can monitor system activity in many other ways.

David Livingstone, Associate Fellow at the International Security Research Directorate, Chatham House, told us that the 'war on cyber crime' was very serious and 'getting worse'. However, GCHQ's [report] published earlier this year reported that a staggering 80% of cyber attacks could be stopped through basic information risk management. Iain Lobban, Director GCHQ, had previously outlined how cyber crime is not just a national security or defence issue but is something which goes to the heart of our economic well-being and national interest. He stated that 'good Information Assurance practice will solve 80% of Government's Cyber Security vulnerabilities. By this we mean observing basic network security disciplines like keeping patches up to date. That, combined with the necessary attention to personnel security and the 'insider' threat, will offer substantial protection for each individual network'.

House of Commons Home Affairs Committee, 2013, 8

The most important point here is that it's not 'the big stuff' that's a problem – most of our organizations will not fall foul of Anonymous (2013) or massive DDoS attacks – the threats we face can largely be defended against by quite simple and routine practices, and at negligible cost, compared to the consequences of a breach.

Firewalls

Firewalls can be implemented in hardware or software, and are a low-level means of keeping network traffic where it is permitted to be. For example, suppose your organization has a network to which all employees' computers are connected. The network may offer access to office software, other software commonly used in the organization (perhaps an accountancy package, or the library catalogue), e-mail, an intranet (web-based content restricted to employees – perhaps an internal directory/calendar) and extranet (web-based content restricted to employees and partner organizations – perhaps a catalogue of products and services) and the internet.

If the organization has an intranet and an extranet, these will be mounted on a web server. The practicalities of handling who should be able to access each are typically managed by a firewall. The firewall will stop attempts which originate outside the organization to access administrative functions on the web server, and will keep intruders from reading the contents of network drives. It may also be configured to prevent employees from accessing certain web services whilst at work (for example, those involving large downloads, or those which would use up bandwidth, such as streaming media).

Firewalls are the first rank of defence for an organization's networks, and must be configured and maintained with care. It will normally fall to an IT department to implement the firewall, but it will often be the information professional's role to decide who should be able to access which resources, or use particular programs.

Websites

Having prevented attackers accessing our web server by physical means, through securing the equipment, and by logging in, through password security and the use of a firewall, we also need to pay attention to the content of a website. In particular, since websites which merely display static content are now unfashionable, we must consider the implications of more interactive website designs. It is important that any feature which allows user input is designed so that it is not possible for attackers to use techniques such as buffer overflow and SQL injection to gain access to content and programs on the server to which they should not have access. Often this will be as simple as designing web forms which only process a restricted range of characters, so that database commands cannot be delivered in the guise of normal input (SQL injection). Sometimes attacks will involve attempts to make user input operate directly on the memory of the system under attack (buffer overflow). In both cases, the remedy is patching the vulnerable software, using patches which can be proprietary or designed in-house. For proprietary software, security alerts and updates should be monitored. For in-house programs and web pages, there are well known steps which can be taken to secure sites – see, for example, wikiHow (2013) – but these may be ignored, partly from a feeling of 'it'll never happen to us'. It will – there are many attackers out there, and the risk is not worth taking.

An associated risk, which is partly due to the 'it'll never happen here' feeling, and partly to laziness, is the use of programs when the default administrator password has not been changed after installation. This is a notorious security loophole, and these default passwords are very well known to the attacker community and, indeed, to anyone who can find the documentation (not very difficult).

Anti-virus, anti-malware, etc.

Anti-virus, anti-spam and anti-malware programs must be kept updated. Unlike firewalls, which operate by examining 'packets' of data primarily to find out where they originate from and where they are going to, these programs compare the contents of files with databases of files which are known to be harmful, hence the importance of keeping the databases regularly updated. Remember that spam is a vector for malware, phishing and Trojans, as described in the last chapter, so reducing the amount of spam that users see should also reduce the chance of security being compromised. Even if someone reacts to spam by using an offer in the message to unsubscribe from the mailing list – 'Click here to unsubscribe from these postings' – using unsubscribe tells the sender that they have reached a valid e-mail address, with a real person reading the mail. This information is itself a saleable commodity, so it may be that the apparently sensible act of unsubscribing – a service which the sender is often bound by law to make – does not in fact reduce the amount of spam you receive. A good spam filter will prevent you seeing the scam, and an address which does not respond will eventually be dropped from the mailing list in any case.

BYOD

BYOD stands for 'bring your own device', and is an abbreviation coined to describe concisely the practice of individuals accessing their organization's resources via a personal hardware device, which at the time of writing usually means smartphones and tablets. However, it is worth noting that the strides made in device development now mean that 'wearable computing' devices such as watches and glasses (e.g. Google Glass) are about to become mainstream consumer devices, and it is very difficult to predict what else may be in development.

BYOD has great benefits for today's worker – the devices are small, easily portable, fashionable and have more processing capability than many desktop machines, especially when used in conjunction with network or cloud services. They are well suited to dynamic working environments, to 'hot desking' and to working on the move. They allow people to access their web resources and e-mail from wherever they happen to be, at any time of day or night, and also make them contactable at any time.

However, smartphones and tablets used to access corporate e-mail are a security risk – they're valuable in themselves, small and portable, so attractive to thieves, and people use them openly in public places, so they're often left on bars, on restaurant tables or in taxis. Unless they're protected by a password-protected screen lock, anyone with access to your phone or tablet also has access to your e-mail account, because the phone or tablet itself handles the password for the e-mail. There was a 16% rise in thefts of personal property on UK railways for the years 2012–2013, and targeting smartphones and tablets is not a practice restricted to the UK.

Data on these devices must be encrypted before they are removed from the workplace. This policy should also apply to USB storage devices, such as data sticks and pen drives or thumb drives. Strong passwords must be set, to prevent access to e-mail and network services. Ideally, an application should be used which can erase the devices remotely in case of loss or theft.

E-mail and attachments, in- and outgoing

Use good e-mail discipline, on your computer and also on mobile phones, smartphones and tablets, because they are another route for malware to get onto your network. Don't open attachments without first checking that they were sent by someone you trust, and even then, it is always a good idea to scan them with your anti-virus program.

Transparency

According to Okhi et al. (2009), Japanese companies that disclose their information security reports are evaluated more highly by others, as was one disclosing an IT risk, prior to an IT accident, compared to another which did not disclose the risk – although both suffered financially, the stock price of the first recovered sooner.

Remember from Chapter 2 that there are legal penalties for not providing data when required to. Nowadays, bad news about organizations spreads very quickly, through social media in addition to the conventional news channels. Cloud-based back-up and business continuity plans can reduce restore times and the associated time it takes to become operational again after a disaster, which again impacts on the reputation, and which is also something that could be disseminated to customers and business partners by the information management department, using social media.

For example, the information management department could well be responsible for maintaining blogs about various aspects of the organization, and communications regarding a disruption to normal service should be considered as part of the business continuity management plan.

Risk

Even if your organization as a whole does not have a formal risk management policy, you should be able to introduce to its information management practices policies including those mentioned above, which will serve to mitigate hazard risks and operational risks, and you should be able to identify these. Opportunity risks would include those concerned with an extension of the organization's activities, and should certainly be considered in any plans for such.

Continuity

As is the case with risk management, the information service should be part of an organization-wide strategy, in this case for business continuity management. If this is not the case, consider what steps it can take to ensure its own continuity, and contribute to that of the whole organization, in the event of disruptions. Since potential causes of disruptions will include the risks identified above, the two are closely interlinked.

....
Exercises

1 Do you have a back-up policy for your own work data? Does your organization have a back-up policy? Which type is it, and who is responsible for its operation?
2 Is your organization accredited under ISO 27001 (Security Management)? Is this used in its advertising? Does it seek accreditation in those with whom it forms partnerships?
3 Is your organization accredited under ISO 22301 (Business Continuity Management), or BS 25999-2 (the older version)? If not, does it have a business continuity plan, or a disaster recovery plan? Can you easily find a copy? When was it last updated?
4 If your business does not have a BCP, draft one, using as headings at least those elements mentioned in the section on risk management.
....

Conclusion

We need to think about security management because of laws and regulations and contracts, and some of these will have requirements which may conflict with one another, especially when the demands of security and privacy are conflicting. There are new requirements for reporting of policies and of breaches, and new legislation coming into operation in the various jurisdictions in which organizations operate means that there is a need for continual review. Security is not an issue that can be considered only in the context of an organization, but is a key factor in its dealings with other organizations and with individuals, whether these be shareholders, customers or connected only indirectly via a third party. 'We also note as a principle, that if personal data is held in any database, no matter how secure, there is a risk of it being accessed inappropriately, either through human error or malice. The only way to ensure data does not leak is not to collect it' (House of Commons Home Affairs Committee, 2013, 9). This is a somewhat fatalistic view to adopt, but it should encourage us to greater vigilance, rather than drive us to despair.

Security responsibilities pervade the organization and its operations. There are corresponding technical demands and practices which must support security, and usually the benefits are unseen, because good practices mean that nothing untoward happens, which is a good thing, but difficult to quantify when advocating expenditure.

Risk management faces similar issues – if it is done effectively, organizations will be successful in offsetting risks by insurance, or avoiding them by improved planning, or dealing with them, again by good planning. Again, the benefits, if seen at all, are seen retrospectively.

Business continuity management is probably the most evident of the management issues considered in this chapter, in that, if it is being practised properly, there will be an ongoing cycle of review and testing. The value is measured simply – continuity of the business in case of disruption – and though we hope that the disruption never occurs, there is an unquantifiable, but substantial, benefit in the assurance that an effective system is in place.

The 'assurance factor' of certification against the relevant standards is again unquantifiable – although enhanced reputation and success compared to others who have not been certified should be an incentive.

Last but not least, it is very important to recognize that none of these standards will be met, and none of the practices and policies adopted, without the efforts of the organization's staff. However worthy the motives behind improving a service, any improvement requires change, and any change requires management. The simple imposition of changes is not fair to staff, who are entitled at least to be kept informed and made part of the decision-making procedure, as far as is possible.

Here, the framework is your friend – frameworks in general demand organization-wide assessment of requirements, risks and impact, and a continual cycle of evaluation and feedback. This is where issues like training in health and safety come into play, and it would be a foolish organization which missed the opportunity to benefit in its planning and evaluation processes from its employees' accumulated experience.

References

Allen, J. H. and Westby, J. R. (2007) *Governing for Enterprise Security (GES)*
Implementation Guide Article 1: characteristics of effective security governance,
Pittsburgh, PA, Carnegie Mellon University.

Anonymous (2013) *Why We Protest*, https://whyweprotest.net/community. [Accessed 01/12/13]

British Standards Institute (2006) BS 25999-1:2006 *Business Continuity Management. Code of Practice*, London.

British Standards Institute (2007) BS 25999-2:2007 *Specification for Business Continuity Management*, London.

British Standards Institute (2013) *Lettergold Plastics Ltd Shows How Certification to ISO 22301 Can Boost Small Firms as Well as Large Organizations*, www.bsigroup.co.uk/Documents/iso-22301/case-studies/BSI-ISO-22301-case-study-Lettergold-Plastics-UK-EN.pdf. [Accessed 01/12/13]

Business Software Alliance (2003) *Information Security Governance: toward a framework for action*, www.entrust.com/wp-content/uploads/2013/05/ITgovtaskforce.pdf. [Accessed 31/10/13]

Constantin, L. (2013) *Oracle Fix Critical Security Holes That Were Open to Hijack Risk*, CIO, UK, www.cio.co.uk/news/security/oracle-fix-critical-security-holes-that-were-open-hijack-risk. [Accessed 23/10/13]

Energy Management Associates (2012) *IBM Endpoint Manager: reaping the benefits of a unified approach to security and it operations management*, Boulder, CO, http://newswires.computing.co.uk/files/amf_incisive_nwires_ps/workspace_7/pdfs/IBMSWGT_241013.pdf?id=0. [Accessed 24/10/13]

Entrust (2004) *Implementing Information Security Governance (ISG): a case study*, Dallas, TX, www.entrust.com/resource/case-study-entrust-and-information-security-governance-2. [Accessed 05/04/14]

Hopkin, P. (2012) *Fundamentals of Risk Management: understanding, evaluating and implementing effective risk management*, 2nd edn, London, Kogan Page.

House of Commons Home Affairs Committee (2013) *E-crime*, London, The Stationery Office.

ISO/IEC (2009a) ISO 31000:2009 *(E) Risk Management – Principles and Guidelines*, http://imeny.comyr.com/file/pdf/ISO-31000.pdf. [Accessed 13/11/13]

ISO/IEC (2009b) ISO Guide 73:2009 *Risk Management – Vocabulary*, International Organization for Standardization.

ISO/IEC (2012) ISO/IEC 27000:2012, Geneva, http://standards.iso.org/ittf/PubliclyAvailableStandards/index.html. [Accessed 30/10/13]

Northwest Controlling Corporation Ltd (2012) *Enterprise Risk Manager™: information security management risk assessment software for ISO 27001/ISO 17799/ISO 27005*, www.noweco.com/itriskse.htm. 'Enterprise Risk Manager™' is a software product and trademark owned by Incom Pty., Australia. [Accessed 28/11/13]

OCLC (n.d.) *Security Whitepaper: OCLC's commitment to secure library services*,

www.oclc.org/content/dam/oclc/policies/security/oclcinformationsecuritywhite
paper.pdf. [Accessed 09/11/13]

Okhi, E., Harada, Y., Kawaguchi, S., Shiozaki, T. and Kagaua, T. (2009) *Information
Security Governance Framework*, WISG'09, 13 November, Chicago, IL,
www.cs.jhu.edu/~sdoshi/jhuisi650/papers/spimacs/SPIMACS_CD/wisg/p1.pdf.
[Accessed 17/11/13]

Price Waterhouse Cooper (2013) *2013 Information Security Breaches Survey: executive
summary*, UK Department for Business Innovation and Skills, www.pwc.co.uk/
assets/pdf/cyber-security-2013-exec-summary.pdf. [Accessed 05/11/13]

Professional Evaluation and Certification Board (2012) *ISO22301 Portal*,
http://pecb.org/iso22301. [Accessed 01/12/13]

US Department of Defense (2007) *Directive 8500.01E Information Assurance (IA) October
24, 2002 Certified Current as of April 23, 2007*,
www.geoffreyanderson.net/capstone/browser/trunk/proposal/research/850001.
pdf. [Accessed 05/04/14]

wikiHow (2013) *How to Secure Your Website: 8 steps*,
www.wikihow.com/Secure-Your-Website. [Accessed 01/12/13]

CHAPTER 6

Frameworks, policies, ethics and how it all fits together

Introduction

So far, we have looked at a variety of functions which information governance performs within the organization. First, there was the area which people normally associate with information governance, if indeed they make any association at all – the part that it plays in complying with legislation. We saw that this is indeed essential, but also that the drive to comply is not, or should not be, the principal, let alone the only, reason for adopting sound information governance and assurance practices.

We considered, in Chapter 2, the Data Protection, Freedom of Information, and Public Records (Scotland) Acts, and the Environmental Information Regulations, all of which are applicable in the UK, and noted that the same, or very similar, legislation is in place or pending in many other jurisdictions. We also noted that the movement of information between jurisdictions is another area for concern. We looked at the importance of adhering to standards in records management, and we have seen that the international standard ISO 15489 has been developed for this purpose.

In Chapter 3, we looked at data quality issues and how they may be managed, and we also considered steps which can be taken to maintain and enhance data quality. Next, in Chapter 4, we examined the threats which could impact on the data we manage and the services we provide, and in Chapter 5 we have set these threats in a greater context of security, as some of the risks which we must manage. The relevant international standard series here is ISO 27000 (information technology – security techniques). We discussed risk management (ISO 31000) as a means of evaluating the different types of risks faced by an organization and the informed decision to transfer, avoid or minimize the effects of risk. Lastly, business continuity planning (ISO 22301) was discussed as a safeguard against the worst consequences of security breaches and equipment failures, amongst other disruptive events which might impact on the information service, as part of the larger organization.

We have a range of elements there, and we have seen their individual importance to the operation of good information governance: so what remains is to contextualize them and fit them together into a picture of what contribution information governance and assurance can make to the total organizational structure.

We have seen some areas in which policy can be developed, and we can now look at the development of an overarching policy, whilst considering the policy statements of relevant professional bodies, and considering their influence. We also need to examine further the ethical dimension and its effect on policy development.

Moving from standards to frameworks

We have seen references to 'frameworks', and the importance that the standards place on developing frameworks against which specific plans can be implemented. In Chapter 2 we saw that the records management framework described by ISO 15489 sets out the characteristics of records, how to organize them, the tools required to do so and the documentation of those management processes. The framework for information security discussed in Chapter 5 laid emphasis on the importance of management involvement in an organization-wide undertaking, and we saw that the Entrust organization was not completely impressed by the framework suggested by the old ISO 17799 standard, because it did not give sufficiently specific guidance on implementation, whereas the ISO 27000 series of standards is more comprehensive.

A risk management framework and a BCM framework are also mentioned in Chapter 5. What do these frameworks do, and how do they contribute to our implementation of standards? Most pertinently, in our current endeavour to understand information governance and assurance, do we need an information governance and assurance framework?

The definition closest to the sense in which we use the term 'framework' in this book was found in Wikipedia:

> Framework is a term describing established practices in a society, science, software development, or hardware design that can be repeatedly applied to solving problems. The problems are solved uniformly (in the same or very similar way) in a framework.
>
> Simple English Wikipedia (2013)

That definition really helps to clear up what these frameworks recommended by the standards are intended to be: 'established practices . . . that can be repeatedly applied to solving problems . . . uniformly'.

Let's look at the content of one of the frameworks we have encountered so far: ISO 15489: *Information and Documentation – Records Management* (ISO/IEC, 2001a; 2001b).

In Part 1, we have a 'general briefing' for 'all staff and management' on 'a framework for best practice' in records management, and in Part 2, a 'framework for records systems', which builds on the best-practice framework. As the term 'framework' implies, we are looking at structures – things which can be built on other structures and in turn can have other structures built on them. The standard for risk management, ISO 31000, provides a useful diagram of its framework (Figure 6.1 on the next page).

We noted in Chapter 5, pages 135–6, that the components from the central box in this figure are the steps which must be implemented in handling risk, but now we see them as the framework on which the implementation (4.4) is constructed. They are preceded by establishing a mandate and commitment (4.2), which we can regard as equivalent to the staff and management briefing we have just noted in the records management framework, and the implementation is followed by monitoring, review and continual improvement, as we should be

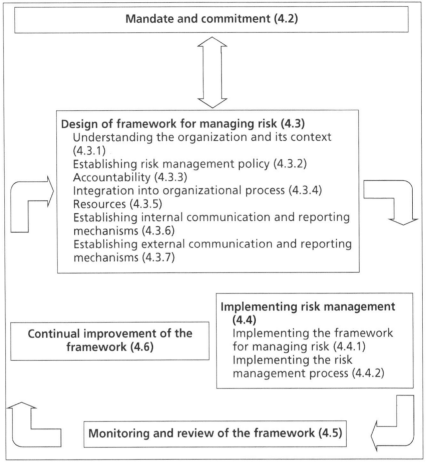

Figure 6.1 Relationship between the components of a system for managing risk (ISO/IEC, 2009, 9)
Permission to reproduce this extract is granted by the BSI.

coming to expect from the cyclical framework (see, for example, Figure 5.2, page 133, the plan-do-check-act cycle).

Figure 6.1 (above) is followed in the standard by the paragraph: 'This framework is not intended to prescribe a management system, but rather to assist the organization to integrate risk management into its overall management system. Therefore, organizations should adapt the components of the framework to their specific needs' (ISO/IEC, 2009).

ISO 27000 (information technology – security techniques) states in section 3.6(b) that a critical success factor in the successful implementation of an ISMS is 'an approach and framework for designing, implementing, monitoring, maintaining, and improving information security consistent with the organisational culture' (ISO/IEC, 2012, 17).

We can see that understanding the organization, or 'an approach . . . consistent with the organizational culture' is a common feature. The design of the framework includes assigning accountabilities, integrating the system into existing processes and setting up lines of reporting, whereby the operation of the system can be monitored internally and external communication and reporting can also be accomplished.

The Data Quality Assessment Framework described in Chapter 3 is concerned with assessing data quality, so the framework defines dimensions of quality, how to measure according to those dimensions and how to process the results. This is roughly a counterpart to 4.3.1 in the risk management framework – having established the mandate and commitment, we now move on, as the first part of establishing the framework, to understanding what we have already.

Hill (2013) argues that since information governance is enterprise-wide, there should be an information governance framework comprising the processes within the organization, the people responsible for implementing procedures and the procedures themselves, which ensure that the organization's information is secure, available, has integrity and can be used with confidence. There should be a team comprising people whose interests span across the organization, from board level to IT, from records management to business units and the legal department. Each of these groups has a different, and complementary, understanding of how information needs to be handled in order for all requirements, from strategic to technical, to be met. The team determines what is done with information belonging to the organization, or which is within its control (remember from Chapter 2 the distinction between a data controller and a data processor). The 'proper use' which the team oversees involves the following of the information governance policies which it has set out and maintains. These policies will include the type of day-to-day issues which we have discussed in each chapter, and can be expanded to encourage the controlled extraction of added business value from the information passing through the organization. So, an information governance framework can help, not only in answering the objectives associated with secure and confidential handling of information, with legislative compliance regarding records and risk and with developing a fitter and more resilient organization with a higher public profile: it can also assist in the development of practices related, for example, to 'data mining' and the processing of 'big data', which exploit to the organization's advantage resources of which it may have been completely unaware.

The existence of the information governance framework, then, means that newer technologies can be actively explored in a planned way, rather than as an ad hoc reaction to some passing crisis. Possible technologies which might repay exploration in our domain of practice include e-discovery, new storage solutions, content management systems, including electronic document and record management systems, and active archiving, where records that are still active but less frequently used are moved from the operational database to storage which can still be accessed quite easily (Hill, 2013).

What is proposed is an overall information governance and assurance framework, endorsed and supported by the executive management, which takes account of all the areas we have discussed that are applicable to the particular organization in question. Since we are discussing organizations in fairly general terms, and we are assuming that the organization has some person, or perhaps a department, concerned with information management, many of the areas we have discussed can be assumed. So, we have a meta-framework, in terms of the Wikipedia definition, a framework of frameworks, each contributing its own element to the structure which provides the complete information governance and assurance package. Just as all organizations produce records in the course of conducting business, whether or not they recognize them as such, so all organizations have a need for information security, and a policy to implement it, even if that amounts to no more than locking away the accounts books at night. Similarly, all organizations face risks, and would at least be well advised to have plans to deal with them, should they manifest themselves as actual threats. It's not quite true, in any case, to say that no one is forcing you to do anything about it – as we have seen in Chapter 5, if your organization is subject to

Sarbanes-Oxley or congruent legislation, there is no choice in the matter.

A business continuity management system is also perhaps something imposed by legislation, but it would seem to be rather rash not to have this very basic planning sorted out, although, as the Managing Director of Lettergold Plastics Ltd observed, and we noted in Chapter 5, it is often assumed in a smaller business that the boss will take care of all these things.

We can say, then, with some confidence, that the elements we have discussed have widespread, if not universal, relevance. It will probably be the case that different organizations need different mixes of the elements, but in general they will need some of each. Our new framework should be designed so that the elements can vary from full-blown certification to international standards to just enough to comply with relevant legislation, and all stages in between. Another way of putting this is that the structure should be modular – modules, each consisting of a framework for a specific purpose (perhaps data quality management) can be 'dropped in' to the overall framework as required by the specific organization, and the modules used might change in response to external environmental factors, such as new legislation (Figure 6.2).

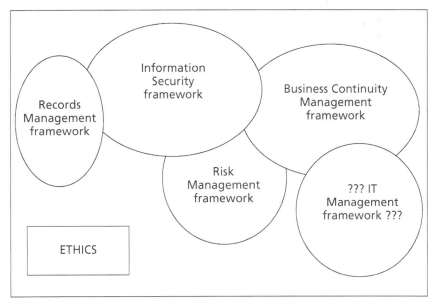

Figure 6.2 All elements are optional, and others (IT, data quality?) may be added

The framework will ensure that the aspects of information governance and assurance that we have considered in this book are at least considered when designing and implementing organizational practices. It may be that some areas are not considered relevant to a particular organization, though, as just discussed, that is probably unlikely. It may be that in some areas standards are used, but not in others, and that is a choice for the organization to make – we shall shortly be considering instances where that may be the case. The important thing from the framework's point of view is that these important areas are considered, and a reasoned response can be given to the question, 'What are your organization's practices regarding . . . (some aspect of information governance)?' If the organization is satisfied, after examining its practices through the lens of the framework, that it has achieved satisfactory assurance regarding its practices, then that is a good outcome. Alternatively, it may be that areas are identified where policies and practices are lacking, or are unsatisfactory, in which case action can be taken to improve those areas.

We begin by looking at an example of a framework where no specific standard was being applied, but where the top level of the organization identified a need for better management of records and greater assurance. A framework 'module' of this type could fill the slot for records management in our meta-framework, or we could employ the ready-made framework from ISO 15489 (records management).

A records management framework – from top-level down

First, we'll describe the 'operational' body in a large and complex organization of agencies. The US National Archives and Records Administration (NARA), in its framework for developing records management guidance, states that it develops 'government-wide records management requirements and broadly applicable guidance', and that it is then the responsibility of federal agencies to develop programs and policies which comply with the requirements and adapt the guidance for their particular programs. NARA 'specify the "what and why"' and the agencies 'provide the "how"' (US National Archives and Records Administration, 2010). We could say that NARA provide the framework, while the agencies look after the implementation. So, for example, NARA requires that agencies identify the records which must be created, maintained and preserved to conduct business, document the activities of the agency and protect the rights of the government and of individuals, employ NARA-approved records retention schedules and address issues arising from the creation of records in new and emerging formats.

NARA is now working under the requirements of a Presidential Memorandum (Obama, 2011) which mandated an 'executive branch wide effort to reform records management policies and practices', because improving records management 'will improve performance and promote openness and accountability by better documenting agency actions and decisions', because NARA 'provide[s] the prism through which future generations will understand and learn from our actions and decisions' and 'to help executive departments and agencies . . . minimize costs and operate more efficiently'. This memorandum takes the place of a standard in our model, in that it begins by stating in very broad terms what the high-level aims are. The memorandum gave each agency 120 days to describe plans, identify obstacles and formulate programs that could assist in reforming records management. It also required the issuing of a directive that agency heads 'take specific steps to reform and improve records management policies and practices within their agency'. This directive (Zients and Ferriero, 2012) set out goals: that the agencies meet targets for managing all records in an electronic format, and that they 'demonstrate compliance with federal records management statutes and regulations'; the latter to include designation of a senior official responsible for compliance, informing all employees of their records management responsibilities, and developing suitable records management training for all staff.

The President's memorandum gave each agency 30 days to designate a Senior Agency Official (SAO), and decreed that within 120 days of that date, the Director of the Office of Management and Budget (OMB) and the Archivist of the NARA issue the directive referred to above.

The 'specific steps' mentioned in the directive, however, are at the level of 'establish records management training', or 'ensure records are scheduled [i.e. that they appear on a record retention schedule]' – the details of implementation are not, yet, very specific, because they are still at framework level. One would expect that, at an agency level, these steps would be further refined, perhaps to describe particular levels of training for certain grades of staff, or to specify retention periods for specific types of document or record series.

Lessons to be learned

What can we learn about implementing frameworks from this example? Firstly, it is a very good demonstration of the power of executive buy-in. The executive in this case is more powerful than most, but only in an absolute sense – within the context of an organization, this is the chief executive. The President's memorandum clearly states good reasons for the action. It sets out objectives that are specific, measurable, achievable, realistic and timebound (SMART). It is clear exactly what must be accomplished, by whom and by when. Areas of responsibility are defined and named organizational roles are identified. A review of plans and programs is required, as well as identification of obstacles. Finally, the authority to carry out actions to reach the stated goals is implicitly delegated.

The reasons given for the action appear calculated to have a wide appeal – greater efficiency, openness, accountability, an appeal to a sense of history and, clinchingly, lower costs. A very clear program is set out, there is no room for misunderstanding, the timescales are short but achievable and the expected results are clear. There is no possibility of mistaking this for an optional exercise, or one which can be 'put on the back burner'. There is a clear end-point at which control over the next stage of the process is handed down to the agencies, because this is a very large structure of organizations, but we can construe 'agencies' as 'departments' within the context of a single organization. In short, this is a model of how to communicate. Whilst this type of edict only works when delivered from the top level, it might be presented *to* the top executives by the information management department as a working example on which to build. The provision of reasons is a particularly important feature – it will be much easier to get people further down the hierarchy to co-operate if they can see the reasons for doing so, and cutting of costs ought to appeal to budget-holders at all levels.

An information security framework – deciding what to implement

Ma, Johnston and Pearson (2008) developed a 'parsimonious framework' for information security, based on objectives and practices found in the literature, in standards and in a survey of 354 certified security professionals. To the three 'traditional' elements of confidentiality, integrity and availability (often expressed as CIA) they added non-repudiation (undisputable evidence that a specific action has occurred), authentication and accountability as objectives and requirements identified by practitioners, academics and security organizations. They then move on to look at practices:

> Without a series of actions or controls used to work towards these objectives, achieving them is merely a matter of chance. However, the complexity of security issues and the number of suggested practices make it increasingly difficult for managers to determine which practices should be implemented.
>
> Ma, Johnston and Pearson, 2008, 255

They drew these practices from 'prominent' checklists – IBM's 88-point security assessment questionnaire, SAFE checklist and AFIPS checklist, as well as ISO 17799, the relevant international standard, described in Chapter 5. When multiple concept items from ISO 17799 were split into their components, this became a list of 56 items. This list was then streamlined, based on responses to the survey of practising security professionals. The 35 'best practices' identified are all 'included or implied' by ISO 17799 (Ma, Johnston and Pearson, 2008, 255). Standards need to be 'boiled down' for implementation – not everything mentioned in a standard will apply in all cases, and there is no need to build into your framework practices which are unnecessary.

Lessons to be learned

This exercise shows that we should not be discouraged from choosing and beginning to implement a framework by the, frankly, intimidating amount that has been published on the subject. We can begin with common-sense, generally agreed objectives, and may well find out that they actually cover a great deal of what needs to be done. The standards themselves are good guides, and although it may take some thought to explore their implications, time spent at the planning stage will be rewarded by effort saved in 'box-ticking' of poorly understood objectives. Remember that a framework is not intended to be a set of specific actions – it is there to be applied in context. We can also learn from this exercise that the frameworks published as part of the standards can be used as a basis from which to develop our own, in-house module, to fit into our meta-framework. Perhaps full standards compliance is inappropriate, or too costly an exercise to undertake at present, but there can be a framework in place which can be used for implementation of good practices, and which could be replaced, should the need or opportunity arise, with the full standards framework.

A risk management framework

There is a potentially stronger incentive towards implementing a risk management framework, in that it may be a legal requirement to do so. If your organization adopts no standards for IT security, or for organizational information security, or for records management, or business continuity, the rest of the world might look on with disapproval, or might refuse to do business with you, but, as long as you somehow manage to escape the attentions of attackers, produce records when required to and protect them otherwise, and as long as catastrophe does not strike, you are allowed to muddle along, as indeed many organizations probably do. However, if your organization is subject to US legislation, or to that of several other countries which have enacted similar legislation, including the UK – in the Companies (Audit, Investigations and Community Enterprise) Act of 2004, for example – then risk management is a requirement, rather than a precaution.

The Sarbanes-Oxley Act

The Sarbanes-Oxley Act of 2002 was introduced in the USA in the aftermath of some very large-scale corporate accounting scandals which had a huge negative impact on share prices and the economy at large. Broadly speaking, the Act mandates transparency and accountability in the accounting practices of public companies. The Act established the Public Company Accounting Oversight Board (PCAOB), which registers and sets standards for auditors. As part of the assessment of internal control on financial reporting (ICFR), company management and the external auditor are required to produce an internal control report which shall

> (1) state the responsibility of management for establishing and maintaining an adequate internal control structure and procedures for financial reporting; and (2) contain an assessment, as of the end of the most recent fiscal year of the issuer, of the effectiveness of the internal control structure and procedures of the issuer for financial reporting.
>
> United States Congress, 2002, 116, stat. 789

The PCAOB auditing standards and the Security and Exchange Commission's (SEC) related guidance for management require management to evaluate company-level controls, perform a fraud risk assessment, and evaluate controls designed to prevent or detect fraud.

COSO

The COSO framework, produced by the Committee of Sponsoring Organizations of the Treadway Commission, is a popular tool used in internal control, and in 2004, COSO published the 'Enterprise Risk Management – Integrated Framework', an eight-component model, comprising:

- internal environment – the 'tone' of the organization
- objective setting
- event identification
- risk assessment
- risk response

- control activities
- information and communication
- monitoring.

Here again, as in Figure 5.2 (page 133), we see the cyclical approach, beginning with an assessment, identification of the objectives which are at risk and the risks pertaining to them, definition of how these risks can be responded to, and a feedback and monitoring element.

According to the New York Stock Exchange, listed companies must have an audit committee, which must, among other requirements:

> discuss policies with regard to risk assessment and risk management . . .
> The audit committee should discuss the company's major financial risk
> exposures and the steps management has taken to monitor and control
> such exposures. The audit committee is not required to be the sole body
> responsible for risk assessment and management, but, as stated above, the
> committee must discuss guidelines and policies to govern the process by
> which risk assessment and management is undertaken.
>
> New York Stock Exchange (2003)

Discussing policies and guidelines is at the framework level, but what the audit committee is required to do, in its assessment of policies with regard to risk assessment and risk management, is at implementation level.

Lessons to be learned

When we look at risk management in the light of the Sarbanes-Oxley Act, we can see that what is desirable is not only the management of risk, but also that the organization is seen to be managing risk, and is assuming accountability, right up to executive level. The use of a recognized framework such as COSO should serve as the badge of a responsible and well prepared organization, and increase the assurance factor for customers, business partners and employees. Risk management may well be required by legislation, but it is a great idea in any case, and worth doing properly.

A business continuity framework – leading practices

Speaking at the 2012 Information Security and Risk Management/IT Conference, Marlin Ness from Ernst & Young identified ten leading practices in business continuity management:

1　Implement a BCM governance model and an enterprise BCM framework.
2　Integrate business impact analysis (BIA) and risk assessment.
3　Leverage emerging technologies such as cloud computing and virtualization.
4　Build for a resilient environment versus a reactive recovery.
5　Understand the true application dependency for recovery assurance.
6　Increase the complexity of testing.
7　Adapt crisis management and communication strategies.
8　Exercise an integrated ERM program.
9　Solicit support from the board of directors and the audit committee.
10　Seek certification and achieve regulatory compliance.

Ness (2012)

This is not a step-by-step model, but rather recommendations of best practice to apply to the BCM process. We have seen some of these points elsewhere, and it is worth noting that the title of the conference includes information security, risk management and IT, whilst the talk is about business continuity. The first two points advocate a single BCM model and framework, clearly defining a methodology, policies and roles – how it is going to work, who is accountable and what mechanisms are in place to make sure that the results of the assessment process are translated into requests for decisions that can be taken by senior management. Impact analysis and risk assessment go hand-in-hand, as our dedication of resources will be dictated by the combined assessment of how likely events are and how much impact they will have.

The third point is that technologies such as cloud and virtual computing give us the opportunity to replicate workload and storage in the cloud, ready to be activated as necessary, and from different physical locations.

The fourth point is that we should aim for success, rather than failure – for an organization which is resistant to risks, and responds appropriately, rather than one which simply prepares for the worst.

The fifth point needs some translation – we need to work out which functions and services are dependent on other services being in place, in order to 'put things back together', especially if some of these services originate outside the organization.

Point six advocates that testing, which is central to good planning, be extended, perhaps to the point of actually moving the organization to its planned 'fall-back' premises, in order to provide a realistic measure of recovery time capability, rather than the hypothetical results from a table-top exercise.

Point seven is that understanding developments in communications technologies means that organizations can keep customers and shareholders informed that the situation is under control and that a plan is in operation, reducing negative impact on the organization's image and the spreading of misinformation.

An integrated ERM program referred to in point 8 means that all types of risk are brought together under a single enterprise risk management program, irrespective of whether they would normally be labelled as 'health and safety', 'security', 'insurance', 'environment' or 'business continuity' risks.

The reference in point 9 to the board of directors and the audit committee should bring to mind the discussion of the Sarbanes-Oxley Act earlier in this chapter. Ness is making the point that things get done more quickly when there is pressure from above, and of course, where applicable, there will also be external pressure on the board and the committee because of the requirement that they individually guarantee that plans are in place.

Finally, seeking certification is, as stated earlier, not just a check that high-quality plans and systems are in place and kept up to date, but also a move towards attaining a badge of which the organization can be proud, and which will enhance its marketability, providing assurance to its customers and business partners.

Lessons to be learned

This is probably the component in which information management is most pervasively involved – it is truly organization-wide, there is a great deal of communication with internal and external entities and reliance on information about internal and external data, events and processes. BCM is an opportunity for the information management department to confirm its position as the nerve-centre of the organization. Ness's ten practices are good examples of features which could be brought in, perhaps individually, to improve gradually on an in-house BCM framework, until finally a decision might be reached to go for certification. The in-house framework can occupy its 'slot' in the meta-framework, doing its job, and being gradually upgraded to full standards compliance.

An IT framework

An IT department will ultimately deliver many of the requirements demanded by the other initiatives to deliver standards compliance within the organization. Large parts of this will fall, partly or wholly, outside our areas of concern – for example, purchasing and phased replacement of equipment is important only insofar as it impacts on reliability and 'uptime'. However, encryption, anti-virus and anti-malware, back-up procedures and firewalls all fall into the information security/risk/continuity area, whereas selection and implementation of operating systems and applications software is somewhere in the middle. The IT department is in the unenviable position of taking the blame for a wide range of systems shortcomings, many of which could be avoided by better use of joined-up thinking elsewhere in the organization. On the other hand, there is often a perception that IT departments work to their own agendas, sometimes to the detriment of the core functions of the organization. The truth no doubt varies from one organization to the next, but it is always advisable to remember that organizations are increasingly reliant on their IT departments in a world of escalating technical complexity, and that they, too, have standards, frameworks and targets to meet.

An IT framework could be one of the optional modules in our 'meta-framework' – whether it would be appropriate to have one depends very much on the place of the IT department in the organization and the relationship between it and information management. It might be found useful to have a module which is actually an interface to the IT department's own framework for applying standards, if it has one in place. This interface would 'hide' the detail of the IT framework's operations from the information governance and assurance (IGA) framework, and would function primarily as a reporting mechanism in the evaluation and feedback stages of the IGA framework cycle.

Lessons to be learned

Many of the suggestions for improved policy set out in the previous chapters cannot easily be implemented without the co-operation of the IT department, if the organization is of sufficient size to have an IT department. Some, or all, may be already in place, and a diplomatic approach will be necessary in order to avoid the suggestion that something as basic as a structured back-up process might not be in place, or that the current one could be improved on. This is where the 'framework' idea can come to our rescue. Certainly, if there is one, it ought to have support from the top levels of the organization, and it ought to include both transparency and a review and feedback process. The assessment part of the framework ought to include an assessment of requirements across the organization, including IT-related or IT-specific areas and the feedback loops ought to take in responses to risks and threats, up to and including disasters, as well as evaluation and feedback about responses to those. Remember, the framework is your friend!

The information governance and assurance framework in operation

A generalized information governance and assurance framework would be multidisciplinary, as we've seen – it would affect IT, information security, records, risk and continuity, at least. Each area requires a review, each requires commitment at the upper levels of the organization, and these are not elements which need to be repeated – they could be done once, for all sections of the main framework. It would be in several stages, beginning and resuming, rather than ending with assessment, because it would be cyclical (Figure 6.3).

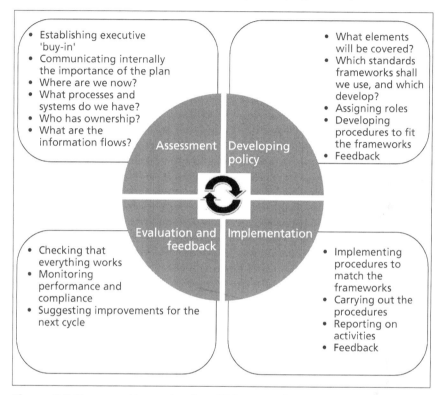

Figure 6.3 The operating cycle of an IT framework

The assessment phase would, initially, establish that there is a will and appropriate backing to drive the rest of the process – the all-important management buy-in. The assessment then proceeds to determine the extent, use and users of information throughout the organization, establishing the business processes in which it is used, the 'owners' at each stage and those who are accountable for the security and integrity of the information. Subsequent cycles through this phase would confirm and, where necessary, update these details.

The next stage would be development of policy, applying across the organization and automated to the greatest extent possible. This stage is influenced by the external environment, and includes elements such as records management, retention schedules, data protection and freedom of information policies and requirements of the Sarbanes-Oxley Act type.

The next stage is implementation, into which modules of a level of complexity to suit the organization can be fitted. These could vary on demand from simple back-up procedures to full ISO compliance. The final component is evaluation and feedback on the operation, although feedback should also take place at each of the stages.

Ethics

It is easy to forget, amidst all the competing demands that handling information places on us, that a common element in all these processes is the fact that they impact on people. It is probably easier to appreciate our ethical responsibilities when handling someone's sensitive personal data, as discussed in Chapter 2, than it is to see our responsibilities to the owners of stocks and shares, whom the Sarbanes-Oxley Act is designed to protect. Freedom of information is an important cornerstone of a modern-day democratic society, and most of those who subscribe to the tenets of such a society would agree that public organizations should be held accountable for their actions. By complying with the relevant legislation, we can do our part to uphold these beliefs.

Environmental information is of concern to all, by definition, and again it falls to the information worker to maintain its availability. Indeed, we would advocate taking an active role in disseminating this information, on ethical grounds as well as for the more practical reasons discussed in Chapter 2.

There is a degree of responsibility placed on those controlling organizations to act responsibly in the interests of their shareholders and their employees, as well as in the interests of others on whom the organization may have an impact. We have discussed in Chapter 5 the importance of the enhanced reputation that an organization can acquire by certification for meeting security standards, and the increased likelihood of other organizations doing business with it, as a result. The best ways to ensure the continued welfare of shareholders, customers and staff involve the continuity and success of the organization, and here risk management and business continuity management, discussed in Chapter 5, come into play.

The CILIP ethical principles

The Chartered Institute of Library and Information Professionals (CILIP), which is the UK professional body equivalent to the American Library Association (ALA) and other national library associations, states its ethical principles thus:

> Library and information professionals are frequently the essential link between users and the information they require. They therefore occupy a position that carries responsibilities.
>
> The conduct of members should be characterised by the following general principles and values:

1. Concern for the public good in all professional matters, including respect for diversity within society, and the promoting of equal opportunities and human rights.
2. Concern for the good reputation of the information profession.
3. Commitment to the defence, and the advancement, of access to information, ideas and works of the imagination.
4. Provision of the best possible service within available resources.
5. Concern for balancing the needs of actual and potential users and the reasonable demands of employers.
6. Equitable treatment of all information users.
7. Impartiality, and avoidance of inappropriate bias, in acquiring and evaluating information and in mediating it to other information users.
8. Respect for confidentiality and privacy in dealing with information users.
9. Concern for the conservation and preservation of our information heritage in all formats.
10. Respect for, and understanding of, the integrity of information items and for the intellectual effort of those who created them.
11. Commitment to maintaining and improving personal professional knowledge, skills and competences.

12. Respect for the skills and competences of all others, whether information professionals or information users, employers or colleagues.

These points are presented in no particular order of priority.

CILIP (2013a)

From these principles, CILIP derive a Code of Professional Practice (CILIP, 2013b), in five sections. Section A is concerned with personal responsibilities, maintaining professional standards of performance and behaviour. Section B relates to responsibilities towards information and its users. It requires transparency and avoidance of bias, confidentiality, fairness, the responsible treatment of intellectual property and concern for the future information needs of society, including preservation and records management.

Section C, 'Responsibilities to colleagues and the information community', encourages responsible and professional behaviour at work, particularly towards colleagues, and encourages the dissemination of the results of research and development projects, with a view to improving services.

Section D is about responsibilities towards society. Here, members are exhorted to consider the public good, promote equitable access, promote skills and knowledge and 'strive to achieve an appropriate balance within the law between demands from information users, the need to respect confidentiality, the terms of their employment, the public good and the responsibilities outlined in this Code' (CILIP, 2013b). Information ethics is not a simple matter of right and wrong.

Section E, 'Responsibilities as employees', again highlights potential conflicts between the 'immediate demands' of an employer and 'the broader interest of the public and possibly the employer themselves'. Members are therefore instructed to promote the legitimate aims of the employer, whilst bringing to the employer's attention any concerns they may have about ethics and legality of practices at work, and avoiding undesirable practices.

It can reasonably be said that this code demands a high standard of conduct, and does not ignore the existence of potentially challenging ethical issues. CILIP has an Ethics Panel which reviews the code and will provide confidential advice to members faced with ethical issues at work. It also notes that 'There are rarely right or wrong answers to ethical dilemmas but more often balances that have to be found between conflicting principles' (CILIP, 2013c).

Other possibly relevant sources when developing your organization's ethics policies are the Association of Computing Machinery's (ACM) Code of Ethics (Association of Computing Machinery, 2013), the Electronic Frontier Foundation (EFF, 2013) and the International Federation of Library Associations and Institutions (IFLA) Code of Ethics for Librarians and other Information Workers (Garcia-Febo et al., 2012).

The role of the information professional in the information governance and assurance framework

As we have seen throughout this chapter, and indeed throughout this book, the information professional's role is a central one, as befits the person whose primary concern is with information governance and assurance, as they have been defined here. From the earliest stages of identifying the need for policies in specific areas of immediate concern, such as records management, to making a case for implementing a framework, to design of the framework, the information professional can offer a uniquely objective approach to matters which might otherwise be unduly influenced by operational concerns. Taking as a professional standpoint the ethical stance embodied in the CILIP code and its analogues, the information professional is in a position to act as a fair dealer in inter-departmental discussions, to trace information flows through business procedures, to suggest roles and responsibilities and to make recommendations for practices compliant with legislation and with standards. At the highest level, selection of standards or other plans for the components of the overall framework, the role would be advisory. The bulk of the work is primarily at the framework level, selecting and designing the best policies, which individual departments would typically implement. Of course, the information management department would be one of these, so there is also implementation work to be done. As the cycle of the framework progresses, as described in the section on the framework in operation (see pages 174–6), a channel for evaluation and feedback would also appear to be an appropriate role for the informational professional to fill.

··

Discussion points

1 You may have noted news stories about organizations' failures in information governance and assurance. How much of an effect do you think this has on their long-term reputation?
2 Do you think that a professional code of ethics, such as CILIP's, should outweigh loyalty to an employer?
3 We have seen that the 'meta-framework' suggested in this chapter is cyclical, a feature it shares with most other frameworks. What time interval or events should trigger another 'round' of the cycle?

··

Conclusion

Throughout this book we have seen the many roles which information serves in our organizations and from the information professional's perspective it is the essence without which the organization cannot operate. In a very real sense, the organization is dependent on effective, efficient and compliant handling of its business records: it cannot operate without its vital records, much of its value relies on the quality and security of its data, and the ability to handle risks and continue in the face of adversity is key to its survival.

In the previous chapters, we have looked at the standards applicable in these areas and at the policy decisions that information professionals can make, in order to have a maximum positive impact on the organization and the conduct of its business, so that those who deal with the organization as customers, as business partners or as staff can be assured that information governance within the organization is one of its key strategic priorities. Sometimes this can be reinforced by certification to a recognized standard and sometimes it will be more appropriate to develop the relevant procedures in-house.

In recognition of the fact that there can be no 'one size fits all' solution, and that each type of organization needs to achieve high performance in information governance and assurance, but in a

different set of areas, a framework has been suggested which would accommodate these differing requirements, whilst serving as a check that the common basic requirements are catered for.

This framework, or 'meta-framework', has spaces which can be filled by appropriate component frameworks selected to apply to a suggested minimum range of areas: records management, information security, risk management and business continuity management. In each case, the framework in question might be derived from an international or other standard, or might be developed by the organization itself. There is also room to expand the meta-framework to encompass other areas and standards, such as ISO 8000 – Data Quality, which might have importance to particular organizations.

The information governance and assurance framework thus has value as a structured way of recognizing and addressing information governance issues, as a review and update mechanism, as an extensible and adaptable tool for dealing with a changing environment and as a central register of the organization's information assurance – a public statement of its responsible and reputable status.

References

Association of Computing Machinery (2013) *Code of Ethics*, www.acm.org/about/code-of-ethics. [Accessed 24/11/13]

CILIP (2013a) *Ethical Principles*, www.cilip.org.uk/cilip/about/ethics/ethical-principles. [Accessed 24/11/13]

CILIP (2013b) *Code of Professional Practice*, www.cilip.org.uk/cilip/about/ethics/code-professional-practice. [Accessed 24/11/13]

CILIP (2013c) *Ethics Panel*, www.cilip.org.uk/cilip/about/ethics/ethics-panel. [Accessed 24/11/13]

EFF (2013) *Electronic Frontier Foundation*, https://www.eff.org. [Accessed 24/11/13]

Garcia-Febo, L., Hustad, A., Rösch, H., Sturges, P. and Vallotton, A. (2012) *Code of Ethics for Librarians and Other Information Workers*, IFLA, www.ifla.org/news/ifla-code-of-ethics-for-librarians-and-other-information-workers-full-version. [Accessed 24/11/13]

Hill, D. G. (2013) *Information Governance: information governance is a necessity*, www.emc.com/leadership/business-view/information-governance-necessity.htm. [Accessed 20/11/13]

ISO/IEC (2001a) ISO 15489-1:2001 *Information and Documentation – Records Management – Part 1: General*, International Organization for Standardization.

ISO/IEC (2001b) ISO/TR 15489-2:2001 *Information and Documentation – Records Management – Part 2: Guidelines*, International Organization for Standardization.

ISO/IEC (2009) ISO 31000:2009 (E) *Risk Management – Principles and Guidelines*, http://imeny.comyr.com/file/pdf/ISO-31000.pdf. [Accessed 13/11/13]

ISO/IEC (2012) ISO/IEC 27000:2012, Geneva, http://standards.iso.org/ittf/PubliclyAvailableStandards/index.html. [Accessed 30/10/13]

Ma, Q., Johnston, A. C. and Pearson, J. M. (2008) Information Security Management Objectives and Practices: a parsimonious framework, *Information Management & Computer Security*, 16 (3), 251–70.

Ness, M. (2012) *Business Continuity Management (BCM): reducing corporate risk and exposure through effective processes and controls implementations*, ISRM/IT GRC Conference, 14–16 November, Las Vegas, www.isaca.org/Education/Conferences/Documents/NAISRM-ITGRC-Presentations/231.pdf. [Accessed 24/11/13]

New York Stock Exchange (2003) *Final NYSE Corporate Governance Rules*, www.nyse.com/pdfs/finalcorpgovrules.pdf. [Accessed 23/11/13]

Obama, B. (2011) *Presidential Memorandum – Managing Government Records*. Washington, DC, Office of the Press Secretary, The White House, www.whitehouse.gov/the-press-office/2011/11/28/presidential-memorandum-managing-government-records. [Accessed 21/11/13]

Simple English Wikipedia (2013) *Framework*. http://simple.wikipedia.org/wiki/Framework. [Accessed 17/02/14]

United States Congress (2002) *The Sarbanes-Oxley Act of 2002*, US Government Printing Office, www.gpo.gov/fdsys/pkg/PLAW-107publ204/html/PLAW-107publ204.htm. [Accessed 23/11/13]

US National Archives and Records Administration (2010) *Framework for Developing Records Management Guidance*, www.archives.gov/records-mgmt/policy/rm-framework.html. [Accessed 21/11/13]

Zients, J. D. and Ferriero, D. S. (2012) *Managing Government Records Directive*, Washington, DC, Office of Management and Budget, National Archives and Records Administration. www.whitehouse.gov/sites/default/files/omb/memoranda/2012/m-12-18.pdf. [Accessed 21/11/13]

Discussion points and exercises

As stated in Chapter 1, there are clear answers to a few of the questions, but most are there to stimulate discussion, and some further points are made about these. Note that these are personal interpretations – don't take them as legal advice, and note that some are, in any case, 'judgement calls'.

Chapter 2

1 You work in the Planning Department of a local authority, and receive a request for any information you hold regarding planning applications by a particular individual for a property at a particular address. What would your response be?

   Although the names of applicants do appear on planning applications, there could be a data protection issue, here, in that the collected applications constitute personal data about the applicant. Local authorities are obliged to make available certain details relating to planning applications, and may choose to do so via the internet. It may be appropriate to direct the enquirer to your register. Under Section 21 of FOIA, you could respond that the information is reasonably accessible by other means. The decision should be made by your records manager.

2 What measures might you take to ensure the security of personal data held by your organization?

   There are many – you might introduce a 'clear desk' policy regarding personal data, ensuring that hard copies are locked away securely when not in use. Personal data taken out of the workplace should be encrypted.

Securely remove or destroy data held on computer equipment which is being disposed of.

3 You work in a hospital, and are asked by the mother of a 14-year-old patient for details about his treatment. How should you respond?

The young person is the person with rights to their information. If you are confident that he can understand his rights, you should respond to any requests by him. In Scotland, the law presumes that a person of 12 years old or more has the capacity to make a Subject Access request. There is no specific age stipulated in Northern Ireland, England or Wales, but the Scottish decision could be taken as a reasonable guideline. However, it would be reasonable to refer the mother to the medical team.

4 As the curator of a military museum, you are asked for details of the service of a named individual who may have served in your regiment at indeterminate dates. How should you respond?

The withholding of information about individuals in service less than 25 years ago has been approved by the ICO under Section 22 of the FOIA, on the grounds that it is due for eventual publication at some future date, and that it is reasonable to withhold the information until that date. In other cases, some information may be personal, and thus exempt from disclosure without the written consent of the individual or his/her next of kin. This is an area in which you could usefully establish a policy.

5 The university in which you are the records manager receives an enquiry about accidents related to harmful chemicals in the last five years. What do you do?

Under the Environmental Information Act, you should log the request and respond in writing within the 20 working day period. The information should be provided unless it would be excessively difficult or expensive to do so, or unless it is exempt from disclosure – for example, if disclosing it would adversely affect national security, or breach the Data Protection Act. It is probable that the data will be readily available, and may well be part of your publication scheme.

Chapter 3

Think of an organization you work for, or have worked for, or an

educational establishment you attend, or have attended. Where might there be data silos? Why might they have arisen? What benefits might be derived from aggregating them?

Anywhere there is a hierarchical structure, with different departments operating at the same level in the hierarchy, there may well be data silos. Even when records are shared across departments, we may find different, and conflicting, versions. A misguided sense of 'ownership' or a perception that job security is improved by 'making yourself indispensable' as the custodian of records may be to blame. A major potential benefit of aggregation is the reduction in redundant and conflicting data.

Chapter 4

Workplace posters are a good, non-confrontational way of getting information across. Design a poster, or a series of posters, explaining how to avoid viruses, worms and Trojans.

Make them colourful, eye-catching and, if possible, humorous. If people mention them to each other, or ask for a copy for their office, you're getting it right.

Chapter 5

1 Do you have a back-up policy for your own work data? Does your organization have a back-up policy? Which type is it, and who is responsible for its operation?

2 Is your organization accredited under ISO 27001 (Security Management)? Is this used in its advertising? Does it seek accreditation in those with whom it forms partnerships?

3 Is your organization accredited under ISO 22301 (Business Continuity Management), or BS 25999-2 (the older version)? If not, does it have a business continuity plan, or a disaster recovery plan? Can you easily find a copy? When was it last updated?

4 If your business does not have a BCP, draft one, using as headings at least those elements mentioned in the section on risk management.

These are fairly straightforward questions, though some of the answers may take a bit of research to find. If the answers are predominantly negative, there may be a case to be made for an information governance and assurance framework. Bonus question: To whom would you best make such a case?

Chapter 6

1 You may have noted news stories about organizations' failures in information governance and assurance. How much of an effect do you think this has on their long-term reputation?
   There are frequent stories of this nature, and it may be that their increasing frequency desensitizes the public, but when other organizations are looking for partners, their memories may well be longer and more critical.

2 Do you think that a professional code of ethics, such as CILIP's, should outweigh loyalty to an employer?
   This may be a question best answered by a series of 'what if' scenarios, to establish where your personal boundaries lie.

3 We have seen that the 'meta-framework' suggested in this chapter is cyclical, a feature it shares with most other frameworks. What time interval or events should trigger another 'round' of the cycle?
   It would probably suffice to have three- or five-yearly reviews, but there will almost inevitably be external events, such as changes in legislation, or internal ones, such as changes in the structure or responsibilities within the organization, which will affect one or more of the component frameworks. Remember, too, that there may well be interdependencies amongst those frameworks, requiring that more than one be reviewed in such an event. The issue of whether reviews are required should be a regular item on the executive board's agenda.

Index

exemptions (*continued*)
  laws and regulations 10
exercises *see* discussion points and
    exercises
external threats 87–100
  bank security awareness 96
  black hats/white hats 96–7
  denial of service (DoS) 93–4
  hacking/cracking 87
  malware 87–93
  Mitnick, Kevin 97
  phishing 94–6
  social engineering 96–100
  white hats/black hats 96–7

Federal Information Security
    Management Act 122
fees
  Environmental Information
    Regulations (EIR) 39
  Subject Access Request (SAR) 34
Financial Services Authority (FSA),
    data quality 73–4
Financial Services Compensation
    Scheme (FSCS), data quality
    73–4
firewalls, policy 102–3, 148–9
flows, information 3–4
FOIA *see* Freedom of Information Act
    2000
frameworks 157–82
  see also standards
  business continuity management
    (BCM) 171–3
  cyclical frameworks 186
  Data Quality Assessment Framework
    (DQAF) 58–9, 161
  defining 159
  information governance 6, 161–4
  information governance and
    assurance framework 174–6,
    179–80
  information security 167–8
  ISO 15489: 159
  ISO 27000 series 160–1
  ISO 31000: 159, 160
  IT 173–5
  'meta-frameworks' 6, 181
  National Archives and Records
    Administration (NARA) 164–7
  records management 164–7
  risk management 168–70
  standards 6, 154

Freedom of Information Act 2000
    (FOIA)
  publication scheme 19–20, 40
  records management 11–12, 15–20
  requirements 16–17
  scope 15–17
  USA 10
Freedom of Information requests 17–19
  exemptions 19
  format of information 18
  mechanism 17
  records management 13
  refusing 18–19
  time for compliance 18
FSA *see* Financial Services Authority
FSCS *see* Financial Services
    Compensation Scheme

glossary xi–xii
Gramm-Leach-Bliley Act 1999: 122

hacking, vs cracking 87
hacking/cracking, external threats 87
hardware
  Bring Your Own Device (BYOD)
    109
  policy 109
hazard risks, risk management 135
Health Insurance Privacy and
    Accountability Act 122
horizontal vs vertical models
  data quality 69–71
  Nestlé 69
House of Commons Home Affairs
    Committee
  cyber crime 147–8, 153
  security 147–8, 153

ICO *see* Information Commissioner's
    Office
Identity Theft Enforcement and
    Restitution Act 2008, threats 101
information
  as an asset 2–5
  vs data 2
  electronic tracing 3
  flows 3–4
  locations 4–5
  restrictions 3
  terminology 2
  tracing 3
  types 3–4
  value indicators 3

Bad Nanny

The Badden Brothers

Maya Nicole